TEACHER-PUPIL RELATIONSHIPS

THE MACMILLAN COMPANY
NEW YORK · BOSTON · CHICAGO · DALLAS
ATLANTA · SAN FRANCISCO

MACMILLAN AND CO., Limited
LONDON · BOMBAY · CALCUTTA · MADRAS
MELBOURNE

THE MACMILLAN COMPANY
OF CANADA, Limited
TORONTO

TEACHER-PUPIL RELATIONSHIPS

BERNICE BAXTER
Co-ordinator of Instruction
Oakland Public Schools
Oakland, California

NEW YORK

THE MACMILLAN COMPANY

1945

TABLE OF CONTENTS

LIST OF TABLES

TEACHER-PUPIL RELATIONSHIPS

CHAPTER I

THE TEACHER'S PART IN TODAY'S EDUCATION

The educational significance of the direct influence of the mature personality of the teacher upon the impressionable personalities of children is worthy of careful evaluation. Especially is this true today. While the teacher's personal example and social outlook have always been factors to be considered, the scope of the teacher's potential influence is greater under the complex living conditions of today than ever before. American schools, and therefore the individual teachers within the schools, are charged with increasingly broadened responsibilities. In recent years public education has assumed functions for which it formerly was not held responsible. These increased responsibilities of the school exact peculiar powers of the teacher. It is only through an appraisal of the widened services of the schools and the demands of a democratic society upon its schools that the teacher's personal part in the educational scheme can be comprehended in its entirety.

American education today is faced with the challenge of having children experience the democratic manner of living. This means that opportunities need to be provided for pupils to learn the principles of democratic life by playing and working together under conditions which foster respect for the rights and privileges of others, tolerance for the viewpoints of other persons, and a sharing of responsibility for decisions affecting the group. It means that children need to grow in an understanding of the balance between freedom and responsibility and between rights and duties. The school, if it is to educate for democratic living, will have to assist each pupil to find his place in the group and to become a contributing member of group enterprise. The pupil must acquire as he matures an understanding of the values of democracy as compared with the values of the various forms of autocracy.

The classroom must be considered a social laboratory in which children learn to live with others cooperatively and harmoniously. It must be a place in which arbitrary decisions are not made, but one in which control evolves from within the group and is exercised for the welfare of the majority. The general atmosphere of this laboratory is characterized by mutual understanding and mutual respect of pupil for pupil, pupil for teacher, and teacher for pupil. There is a purpose-sharing attitude expressed by all members of the class, the teacher included. Since the teacher is the one adult member in the group, his every act has to coincide with the democratic way of thinking and acting which he would have pupils acquire. The teacher cannot give lip service to democracy but must exemplify democratic ideals if he is to inspire children to democratic living.

Today's education makes another very realistic demand upon the teacher, that of teaching pupils to adjust to changed conditions. With the technological advances which have been made in the past few years, it is not possible to foresee future living conditions and to prepare for them. The school must teach children to expect change, to adjust to new conditions, and to meet the unexpected. Discussion regarding change will not insure a readiness for meeting new conditions. Children will have to know through experience what it means to face an unfamiliar situation and to adjust to it. They can learn to reason by analogy and to imagine the influences and effects of new inventions, but they will not acquire the emotional and physical resiliency that adaptation requires if they do not have many opportunities for experiencing change. The teacher is not only the mentor and guide in shaping the experiential environment, but must have an understanding of social progress and social purposes. He must be able to distinguish enduring values from transitional phases of development and must be a flexible and open-minded person himself. The teacher who has failed to keep in tune with modern living is not much help to pupils in aiding them to discriminate between that which is lasting and that which is momentary and fleeting.

The changing social situation has affected conditions under which children live today. It is no longer generally true that the home is the social institution in which children learn the necessity for co-operative enterprise, with the several members of the family contributing their energies to the support and comfort of the family group. Urban life and industrial specialization have caused home life to become definitely altered. Gradually, the school has assumed responsibility for aspects of training which formerly were the concern of the home. The classroom has become the place where social enterprise is fostered. No longer is the school entirely concerned with the transmission of the social culture as was the case years ago. The school to an increasing degree is becoming the center for the kind of group participation formerly true of the home.

The teacher in today's school is no longer the channel through which mere information flows, but is responsible for planning experiences for children which will be educative in many ways; in the seeking and finding of information; in sharing findings with others; in accepting the substantiated information presented by others; in working in the capacity of both leader and follower; in deciding worth-while group projects; and in finding ways and means of solving problems and of sharing both the work and the results of work with other children. Perplexing problems of a social nature earlier restricted to the home are now being met in the school if the teacher has the foresight, initiative, and ability to plan and direct these social undertakings for her pupils.

Modern life, because the tempo is rapid and conditions constantly changing, makes heavy demands upon children's emotional and physical reserves. Mental hygienists agree that the school plays an important part either in helping to conserve mental, physical, and emotional energy or in causing it to be dissipated. While much of the physical well-being must be entrusted to the home, the school must be an active agent in providing for the physical-growth needs of each individual child. If the teacher is aware of the bodily-growth needs of children and knows how to avoid eye and other muscle strain, to prevent fatigue, and to provide a program of balanced activity and relaxation, unnecessary physical exertion with its possible harmful results may be averted. This can be accomplished only if the teacher is conversant with the out-of-school life of pupils and plans school activities which build for balance in the physical life of each individual pupil.

Children have emotional needs which require particular attention and sympathetic understanding. Under the pressure of group action these needs become intensified and more complex in nature. Every growing child needs to feel his own worth and developing power. He needs recognition and encouragement. Only as he accepts and understands himself does he function at his best. Fears and inhibitions concerning himself. and inability to direct his attention to external conditions detract from his well-being and happiness. The teacher must understand this need for recognition and so shape events that every child has sufficient successful experience to insure a sense of security and worth.

The approval and acceptance of others give the child the feeling of importance which everyone craves. To have his efforts approved and accepted will encourage a child to greater endeavor, at the same time strengthening his regard for himself and for those approving of him. However, continuous and uninterrupted approval may be damaging. Every child needs to learn his limitations and inabilities and to adjust to them without becoming unduly disturbed. The teacher must know how far to let affairs take their course in order to reveal to children their shortcomings and inadequacies without sacrificing their self-confidence and their feeling of status in the group.

There is agreement among educators that it is education's task to foster the integration of each individual personality while assisting the individual to find his satisfactions in solving problems of worth not only to himself but also to his immediate group and eventually to humanity at large. This presupposes on the part of the teacher a sympathetic understanding of the behavior tendencies of different age levels and of what constitutes appropriate and zestful experiences for each level. It further presupposes an understanding of the way in which learning takes place and of the environmental influences which induce learning. The teacher must be so thoroughly acquainted with each child that the child is guided into tasks which he can accomplish with some degree of success. Only by seeing the worth of his own efforts can an individual acquire that con, fidence which is necessary for successful enterprise un, der present-day living conditions. Every child should be acquiring information and facts, but, in addition, he must know how to use facts and to work through such problems as present themselves.

It is evident that today's education requires the teacher to be the informed, well-integrated, and far-seeing adult member of a children's community. It is no longer enough that the teacher be the possessor of knowledge. Today's teacher must be a "social engi-neer" capable of setting up a provocative environment for children's learning, charting the course of each in-dividual child through the ever-changing social rela-tionships in which he is involved and assisting each pupil to grow in his understanding of himself and of others. American education prescribes further that the teacher be responsible for teaching children to respect the personalities of others and for teaching them to work and play co-operatively with others under restric-tions and privileges established and maintained by majority will.

The challenge to education and to teachers as out-lined is one of great magnitude. The general prepara-tion for such teaching requirements should be broad. The teacher needs a liberal education and should be both a student of the world's culture and a student of the sciences, particularly of those sciences which afford insight into human behavior and growth. Teaching requires scholarship, mental ability, and genuine delight in the pursuit of knowledge, but above all else teaching demands a human being who is capable of establishing rapport with children and who personally is worthy to be an influencing factor in the environment in which children are growing and to which they are reacting.

Programs of teacher education have been expanded to afford more thorough and more adequate preparation for the demands which have been prescribed. Attention has been given to the selection of candidates for teaching. Institutions devoted to teacher preparation have concerned themselves with the personal and social fitness of candidates for their increasingly complex duties. Notwithstanding the effort and time which have been expended, there remains a definite need for further investigation of the teacher's part in the teaching-learning process. Discriminating selection and appropriate experiences for improving teacher preparation will take place only as there is more specific understanding of the teacher's effectiveness in stimulating pupil behavior consistent with the expressed aims of American democratic education.

Several years ago the writer undertook to study the effectiveness of teacher personality by observing teacher-pupil relationships. It had been evident through experience that pupils' successful orientation to school life and through school life to social life in general was influenced by the teacher's insight and personal ability to promote in pupils a feeling of well-being. If a pupil's classroom relationships were such as to assure him of acceptance of himself by others and of the worth of his efforts, he seemed to be well on the way toward behavior which should prove satisfying both to himself and to his group. Why some teachers accomplished this while others failed was a matter of conjecture. Close, consistent observation of teachers who were effective in eliciting constructive social conduct from children gave promise, therefore, of revealing some details of behavior not apparent to the casual observer.

Six teachers were selected first for observation and study. Several months were spent in observing and recording happenings in the classrooms of these teachers. The diary records of the observed behavior of the six teachers and their pupils made possible a somewhat complete description of each teacher's personality in terms of her influence upon pupils' reactions. The study of the six teachers served to validate a procedure which was used later in the observation of relationships in thirty-six additional classrooms.

The remaining chapters of this book are devoted to an account of the observational method which was used and the findings which resulted. It is the hope of the writer that the descriptions of effective teachers may prove helpful to the teachers in service as well as to those interested in the preparation and selection of teachers. Young persons who are anticipating teaching, too, may find in the pages which follow a depiction of the composite personality requirements of the successful teacher.

At the outset, however, it may be well to mention that there is no one pattern-personality which the writer has discovered. As the chapters of the book are read, it should be apparent that no one teacher possessed all of the characteristics which were found to contribute to good teaching. The one teacher who is selected for detailed description in Chapter V was chosen because the growth process of the teacher as a person as well as the responses of children to her were more open to view than in the case of any other teacher. The study of the forty-two teachers revealed the need for responsiveness, adaptability, and personal resiliency in teachers rather than the possession of any set of exact or particularized characteristics. Nothing that is said in the subsequent chapters should be construed to mean that all successful teachers are describable in identical terms. This caution is expressed with the hope that it will be kept in mind while one reads the attempted description of teachers. The very nature of the teacher-pupil relationship being active, it would be erroneous to imply that such interaction can be described as a static or definite entity.

CHAPTER II

OBSERVATION OF TEACHER-PUPIL RELATIONSHIPS

Undoubtedly every experienced judge of teaching and every alert teacher is more or less aware of the interaction of personalities in the classroom. Most teacher-rating scales include items for checking or describing the teacher's personality. Professional literature is replete with discussions and dissertations on the subject of teacher personality. Of late, particular educational emphasis has been given to the analysis and to the clarification of qualifications essential to teaching success.

Numerous studies, too, have been made in attempts to discover how years of preparation, grades earned in college, years of teaching experience, and measures of physical and mental aptitude correlate with judgments of teaching success. These studies have yielded some results of a significant nature. In general, however, it may be said that the one and only predictive measure of teaching ability which has been found reliable is that of actual practice teaching. The correlation is high between grades in practice teaching and teaching itself. This would indicate that the one valid way to estimate a teacher's true worth is to know the personal effect of that teacher upon learners.

Two teachers may possess similar knowledge in a given field, be equally impressive in dealing with adults, and well matched in measured mental and social maturity, but radically different in the effect they have upon children. One may stimulate learning to a much greater degree and arouse in children more constructive social attitudes than the other. To the casual observer of these teachers there may be little difference in their teaching. The reason for the difference in teaching effectiveness may not be found in the pupils' ability to comprehend that which is to be taught nor in the teacher's facility of expression, or ability to make lucid and clear explanations, nor in any of the usually listed items which characterize good teaching. The receptivity which the teacher as a person arouses in pupils is often referred to as an inborn quality. The frequent use of the term "natural-born teacher" testifies to the acceptance of this general idea. A desire to investigate this receptivity-producing effect of the teacher upon the pupil prompted the writer to attempt a detailed study of teacher-pupil relationships. Since other efforts to analyze the teaching act have failed to reveal the specific behavior which differentiates exceptional from mediocre teachers, it was hoped that observation of teachers in action might throw some light upon the "teacher ingredients" which produce pupil responsiveness.

It was encouraging to find, as a preliminary to the actual observation in selected classrooms, that teachers and principals in cities geographically far apart were in agreement regarding evidence which was indicative of an interacting relationship between teachers and their pupils. A brief questionnaire, a copy of which appears on page 14 was sent to four groups of teachers of varying experience to ascertain if there were any specifics of teacher-pupil interacting behavior which were recognizable by teachers. The groups are indicated at the bottom of Table I on page 15 in which summarized responses to the questionnaire are given. In the Appendix on pages 165-166 a description of the personnel of each group will be found. There were included in the four groups teachers and principals whose professional preparation and experience differed widely.

No directions other than those appearing on the questionnaire were given. Only such examples as are cited were included. The reason for restricting directions to the minimum was the avoidance of too much suggestion. Since the purpose of sending the questionnaire was to discover whether there were evident teacher-pupil relationships upon whose significance some agreement might be expected, every attempt was made to avoid influencing those responding to the questionnaire. Also, it being the purpose of the questionnaire to discover whether behavior characteristics were sufficiently overt to impress unselected observers in somewhat the same way, it was necessary to solicit an undirected response.

EVIDENCES OF PUPIL-TEACHER RELATIONSHIP

Explanation: There are evidences of the interaction of teacher and pupil personalities in every classroom. The effectiveness of the teacher is often judged on the basis of observable evidences of this interplay of personalities.

Will you please list significant evidence such as an observer might *see* in a classroom. The following is presented as the form to follow:

PUPIL	Reciting, looking directly at teacher	TEACHER	Smiling, nodding approval
PUPIL	Scowlingly and haltingly handing something to teacher	TEACHER	Holding out hand. Body rigid and tense

As a check upon a possible personal bias being read into the responses to the questionnaire, two professionally experienced persons were asked to assist in tabulating the received returns. The questionnaires were read and tabulated by three individuals working together. Since listed pupil-teacher relationships were so clearly and explicitly stated, the three tabulators found little difficulty in grouping together responses of a similar nature.

Table I indicates the categories under which the responses were organized and the number of persons in each group submitting responses which fell under the respective categorical headings. It is significant to note that of the twelve hundred two responses, one hundred eight, or almost nine per cent of the total number were sufficiently similar in character to be arranged under one heading. Slightly over sixty per

TABLE I

TABLE OF TABULATED RETURNS OF QUESTIONNAIRE ON PUPIL-TEACHER RELATIONSHIPS

PUPIL	TEACHER	FREQUENCIES				
		*1	*2	*3	*4	Totals
1. Disturbs either intentionally or unintentionally—does not do expected thing—makes error	By posture, gesture or facial expression calls attention to pupil's shortcoming	27	30	39	12	108
2. Happy, eager, enthusiastic, interested and co-operating	Alert, cheerful, enthusiastic, helpful, vivid facial expression	47	38	10	8	103
3. Nervous, shy, timid, hesitant, stammering	Helpful, leisurely, calm, unruffled, patient, soothing	39	28	7	22	96
4. Brings in something of interest	Shows interest, commends and shows to class	27	21	19	18	85
5. Accidentally breaking something, not complying, making an error	Showing disapproval, correcting firmly and decisively	38	15	17	15	85
6. Obstinate, sullen, refusing to work, disgruntled	Impatient, losing temper, fault-finding, curt, sarcastic	19	10	11	7	47
7. Reading haltingly, nervous, uncertain, late in complying	Impatient, critical, nervous, tapping foot nervously	38	11	0	8	57

*1 San Francisco State Teachers College Teachers.
*2 Supervisors, Principals, and Teachers from San Francisco Bay Region.
*3 Demonstration Teachers, New Haven Schools, Connecticut.
*4 Teachers, W.M.D. Hartford School, Connecticut.

TABLE OF TABULATED RETURNS OF QUESTIONNAIRE
ON PUPIL-TEACHER RELATIONSHIPS (*Continued*)

PUPIL	TEACHER	FREQUENCIES				
		*1	*2	*3	*4	Totals
8. Accidentally spills or breaks something	Understandingly overlooks, helps, or shows consideration	34	12	2	4	52
9. Omits courteous answer, forgets to do that which is expected, makes error in speech	Draws attention to omission by giving omitted answer, exhibiting surprised or questioning look	0	0	41	7	48
10. Reciting in unsure, halting manner	Impatient, critical, strained or bored looking	12	28	0	4	44
11. Disturbing or interrupting	Stops, awaits attention, and then proceeds	20	4	12	6	42
12. Nervous, talkative, restless, disorderly	Voice shrill, using many words and gestures, scolding	13	21	1	0	35
13. Disturbs by being noisy, overly enthusiastic, transgressing	Demands restitution by assignment of punishment, does not enter into child's enthusiasm	6	14	13	2	35
14. Students working concentratedly	Helping individuals calmly and in a devoted businesslike way	4	25	0	6	35
15. Shows friendly, confident spirit— as coming in to greet teacher, asking a question	Responding eagerly and graciously to his approach	0	23	3	0	26

TABLE OF TABULATED RETURNS OF QUESTIONNAIRE
ON PUPIL-TEACHER RELATIONSHIPS (*Continued*)

PUPIL	TEACHER	$*1$	$*2$	$*3$	$*4$	Totals
16. Attention wandering, daydreaming	Tries to enlist attention in new task	12	6	0	7	25
17. Speaks loudly, calls out in over-enthusiastic way	Uses soft voice, beckons or by gesture suggests quietness	0	5	7	11	23
18. Tries to monopolize, shows off—waves hand insistently	Ignores, lowers hand, quietly dismisses	0	10	13	0	23
19. Crying child wants to go home—disturbed over imagined wrong	Directs attention to some object or other interest, ignoring complaint	0	5	8	9	22
20. Working happily, following directions, confident (voice well modulated)	Decidedly clear in directions (voice well modulated)	0	10	1	12	23
21. Needing help in solving a problem	Commending effort, giving needed help	0	13	3	5	21
22. Pushing—slow in complying	Resorts to physical correction, impelling	11	4	1	3	19
23. Disorderly, talking, throwing objects, no purpose	Ignoring happenings, preoccupied, unprepared, not guiding	4	12	1	0	17

FREQUENCIES (heading above the $*1$ $*2$ $*3$ $*4$ Totals columns)

TABLE OF TABULATED RETURNS OF QUESTIONNAIRE ON PUPIL-TEACHER RELATIONSHIPS (*Continued*)

PUPIL	TEACHER	*1	*2	*3	*4	Totals
24. Tells funny incident, enjoying it as he tells it	Enjoys fun with class	o	5	7	o	12
25. Gives teacher present	Receives it graciously	o	11	4	o	15
26. Seeks undue attention	Impatient, scolds, refuses to give attention, sarcastic	2	o	4	8	14
27. Students helping teacher or one another	Nods approval or commends encouragingly	o	14	o	o	14
28. Attentive and respectful in receiving correction, promising to do better	Calling attention to mistake kindly, pointing out needed improvement	o	2	8	4	14
29. Uninterested	Explaining at great length	5	8	o	o	13
30. Working carelessly	Commends carefulness of others	o	o	5	3	8
31. Seeking help hopefully	Resentful of interruption	o	6	o	o	6
32. Takes advantage of teacher's absence	Leaving class to own management	o	6	o	o	6
33. Showing disapproval	Imposing own choice on an activity	4	o	1	o	5

The FREQUENCIES header spans the columns *1, *2, *3, *4, Totals.

TABLE OF TABULATED RETURNS OF QUESTIONNAIRE
ON PUPIL-TEACHER RELATIONSHIPS (*Continued*)

PUPIL	TEACHER	*1	*2	*3	*4	Totals
		FREQUENCIES				
34. Attends to work while teacher is out of room	Leaving class to its own devices	0	5	0	0	5
35. Disagreeing with teacher	Listens politely, giving source of information	0	0	4	0	4
36. Makes mistake, cheating by intent or unintentionally	Overlooking, but suggesting a "better way"	0	0	0	4	4
37. Leaves work reluctantly	Reprimands with "Come at once!"	0	0	2	0	2
38. Children talking loudly	"Stop!" with authority but not crossly	0	0	2	0	2
39. Brings gift	Indifferent	0	0	2	0	2
40. Breaks window—reports directly	Approvingly commends in direct way	0	0	0	1	1
41. Tactfully corrects teacher	Gratefully receives criticism	0	0	0	1	1
42. Makes mistake	Calls upon another child to tell child of his mistake	0	0	1	0	1
43. Children watch with wonder and surprise	Carries pocketbook around in front of pupils, watching them suspiciously	0	0	1	0	1
44. Tearful, penitent	Pleading for him to do his best	0	0	1	0	1
	Totals	362	402	251	187	
	Grand total					1202

cent of all the responses could be grouped in ten categories.

Experience with the questionnaire indicated that teachers in geographically separated localities were aware of the same indications of the interacting behavior of pupils and teachers. Attached notes and letters indicated that those answering the questionnaire were interested in knowing what use was to be made of their answers. They expressed a desire to know the results of any anticipated study of teacher-pupil relationships, registering an affirmative attitude toward the potential value of an investigation dealing with the implications of such relationships.

Encouraged by the understanding participation of the two hundred twenty teachers and principals responding to the questionnaire, the next step was to test out the objectiveness with which observations could be made. The assistance of three persons experienced in judging teaching effectiveness was secured. A series of trial observations was made for the purpose of discovering to what extent the experimenter's judgment regarding significant classroom happenings could compare with that of the three co-operating observers.

The process of observation was simple. The experimenter and one of the assisting observers entered a classroom for the purpose of recording, either while in the classroom or immediately afterward, what each considered the prominent features of the classroom situation. In other words, each attempted to judge the most vital and salient characteristics of the classroom proceedings and briefly record them.

The number of classes observed by the experimenter and each of the assisting observers varied. There was no attempt made to regulate either the number of classrooms visited nor the time spent in each classroom. The object of this preliminary observation was solely to ascertain the extent of agreement between the judgments of the experimenter and those of three others who were thoroughly experienced in observing classroom procedure.

In each case the experimenter and the observer assisting would enter a classroom, later record the significant features observed, and then discuss their recordings in a short conference. The last was done in order to explain explicitly the written record. Upon the completion of observation in the centers the recorded data were submitted to two other experienced supervisors of classroom instruction. These persons assisted the experimenter in a tabulation which would indicate points of similarity and dissimilarity between the observer's recordings and those of each of the assisting observers. The summarized results are as follows:

Observer One and the experimenter agreed on twenty-five items regarding conditions in seven classrooms and disagreed on five, an eighty-three and one-third per cent agreement.

Observer Two and the experimenter agreed on thirty-five items regarding eleven classrooms and disagreed on seven, an eighty-three and one-third per cent agreement.

Observer Three and the experimenter agreed on twenty-five items regarding six classrooms. They disagreed on none.

These results made the observer feel that if her judgment corresponded to the extent to which it did with three individual judges each of whom was familiar with the teachers and pupils concerned, further preliminary practice was unnecessary.

The trial observations substantiated the impression gained from tabulating the questionnaire responses, namely, that there were obvious evidences of teacher-pupil behavior which were observable and recordable and which an experienced observer could discern without prejudice. It seemed timely and appropriate, then, to attempt an intensive and prolonged study of a few carefully selected teachers. Consequently, six teachers were selected by a group of competent judges for thorough study and observation. The personal relationships within these six classrooms became the object of regular and sequential observation.

For a period of five to six months the happenings in these classrooms were observed and recorded, but only those were considered which gave a cameralike account of the teachers' behavior and the resulting

pupil behavior or the reverse cause-and-effect interacting behavior. Due to the frequency of visits and the
long period of time over which the visits extended both
pupils and teachers gradually came to disregard the
observer's presence, a condition which made possible
a recording of natural and usual happenings uninflu-
enced by the presence of a second adult in the classroom. The absence of strain and self-consciousness on
the part of teacher and pupils made it possible for the
observer to converse freely with the children and with
the teacher when opportunity permitted. Thus not
only the observations but these conversations served
as source material for more accurate interpretation of
the interplay of personalities.

As a rule, observations were recorded immediately.
Thus a complete diary record was kept for each classroom situation. Length of observation time varied
with conditions within the classroom. Since the purpose of the study was to see conditions as they naturally
existed, visits were shortened or lengthened to preserve rapport between the teacher and the observer.
All details pertaining to each visit were kept in a
time sequence with length of period of observation as
well as the character of work in progress. Each observational record was complete in itself but with some
accounting made of intervening events if the same
were necessary for a better understanding of that
which was observed.

By keeping a sequential record it was possible to

compare the early half of the observations made with the later half. This was done by analyzing the complete diary record of each classroom and placing specific observations of like character under headings or captions describing the teacher. By dating the specific instances of teacher-pupil behavior and arranging them in chronological order the agreement between the early and later observations was apparent.

Table II shows the distribution of the specific instances of significant teacher-pupil behavior for the early and later halves of the observation period.

TABLE II

TABULAR ARRANGEMENT OF RECORDED PUPIL-TEACHER
RELATIONSHIPS ACCORDING TO NINE APPLIED
DESCRIPTIVE ITEMS—EARLY HALF AS
AGAINST LATER HALF

TEACHER	ONE		TWO		THREE		FOUR		FIVE		SIX	
Halves	Early	Later	Early	Later	Early	Later	Early	Later	Early	Later	Early	Later
Item 1	11	11	3	5	8	13	1	4	4	6	13	8
Item 2	2	3	4	2	8	6	1	3	4	2	4	5
Item 3	12	2	7	2	7	2	8	2	1	3	2	1
Item 4	2	2	6	7	7	8	7	3	3	3	5	6
Item 5	7	8	2	2	5	4	3	3	1	8	5	4
Item 6	4	5	4	3	3	2	1	0	10	0	1	2
Item 7	8	6	2	2	2	2	2	1	0	4	6	1
Item 8	2	8	1	1	0	3	0	5	2	2	0	2
Item 9	1	4	3	4	—	—	—	—	1	2	0	5
Totals	49	49	32	28	40	40	23	21	26	30	36	34

As a further check upon the reliability of the observations made, some assistant observers were invited to make sample observations in the classrooms while the regular observations were in progress. There was close agreement between these and those recorded in the diary records.

This intensive and comprehensive study of the six teachers gave ample proof of the fact that there were certain definable teacher-pupil relationships which existed in each of the six classrooms. The relationships were not transitory and fleeting but occurred with consistency and sufficient regularity to be used in characterizing each of the teachers studied.

Teacher One was dramatic and playful with children, ingenious in utilizing opportunities for teaching, interested in children as persons, optimistic and constructive in comments and manner, original and different in conversation, but was definite and businesslike in exacting pupil accomplishment after she had planned with them as to what they were to do. This teacher was courteous and kindly in her dealing with children. The children were considerate of one another and appreciative of one another's accomplishments. They worked concentratedly and with apparent interest under the careful guidance of the teacher.

Teacher Two was a quietly enthusiastic teacher, who possessed an evident sense of humor and was free from inhibiting restraints. She, too, was conversational, and friendly in tone and manner but was more interested in having pupils direct their own conduct than conform to her plans for them. This teacher was able to guide many simultaneous activities with poise and without evidence of strain. She was particularly interested in the out-of-school life of her pupils and possessed insight into children's emotional and physical needs. There was a naturalness about the pupils in this room. Their standards of conduct and accomplishment were self-imposed, that is, they with the teacher had set up their own goals and assumed joint responsibility for results. They, like the teacher, were free and uninhibited in expressing their own opinions.

Teacher Three showed an eagerness to be kind and helpful to her pupils. She was lacking, however, in her ability to evaluate pupils' efforts and was easily distracted from what she started to do. The pupils in her room took advantage of her confusion and did not conform to her requests. Her bewilderment stirred her pupils to noisy, erratic conduct, and in turn their disorder seemed to distract her to complete loss of control. She resorted to threats and then to cajoling but to no avail. Lesson periods became for the most part veritable riots.

Teacher Four was kind and thoughtful in her relations with her pupils. She lacked spontaneity and enthusiasm and thought that children should learn to work hard. Her pupils were orderly, submissive, and restrained, reflecting the teacher's seriousness of purpose. This teacher recognized abilities and limitations and adjusted her instruction to meet individual needs, but her entire program was teacher-directed. Children in this room responded apathetically and with hesitation.

Teacher Five was dominating and imposing, entirely oblivious of pupil initiative and resourcefulness. Her voice was loud and harsh and her manner aggressive. Pupils in this teacher's room were industrious and hard-working but showed little self-direction. The teacher's expressed aim was to have children learn. She was proud of her pupils' accomplishment as were they. The pupils, like the teacher, were boisterous and harsh but not unfriendly to each other. Each applied himself with obvious effort to tasks assigned by the teacher.

Teacher Six was habitually quiet, poised, and courteous in her relations with pupils. She possessed a self-restraint in permitting to children freedom of movement and speech and was more interested in thoughtful responses from children than in perfect routine. She was keenly alert to the needs of the children and knew the limitations and capabilities of each. The children in this room were self-directed, knew where to find materials, and evidenced the same thoroughness and quiet persistence in working which characterized the teacher.

In brief, the prevailing teacher-pupil behavior in each classroom was describable as follows:

Teacher One —A relation of mutual harmonious and appreciative responsiveness.

Teacher Two —A relation characterized by a mutually intelligent evaluation of each other's contribution to the classroom situation.

Teacher Three—A relationship in which understanding of a common purpose was conspicuously lacking.

Teacher Four —A relationship of mutually dull conformity to routine.

Teacher Five —A relationship dynamic in nature, of aggressive, driving harshness in the acquisition of facts to be learned and exhibited.

Teacher Six —A relation characterized by eager participation in mutually understood and enjoyed activities.

The observation of this limited number of teachers indicated that teacher behavior does have a definite influence upon pupil behavior. There were decided similarities in the reactions of pupils and their teachers. The six teachers tended to stimulate pupils to the same kind of behavior which they exhibited.

Tenseness on the part of one teacher begot tenseness in the children she taught. The relaxed and unhurried manner of another teacher was duplicated in the ease and calmness with which pupils in that room went about their work. The care and painstaking attitude of a third teacher was characteristic of her pupils although those pupils were but seven and eight years of age and not particularly able children. A fourth teacher who worked with driving intensity stirred children to the same blind application as that with which she worked. The persistence over a period of months of this similarity of conduct in teachers and pupils indicated that the teachers observed were having a pronounced and definite effect upon the behavior of children, at least while the children were in contact with the teachers.

The fact that the majority of children in a given classroom were being molded into the behavior pattern of the teacher testified to the influence of the teacher's personality upon pupil behavior. While the weaker teachers were failing to get from children the responses that they wanted, they were getting responses that coincided with their own behavior. The teacher who was ineffectual and easily disturbed or distracted had her efforts rewarded with inattention rather than attention from pupils. Her whole class became disorganized and unruly with her own disintegration. The more adequate and better integrated teacher had a few children who had not learned to work with the group, but they were in the minority and recognized as variants by the other children in the room who were undisturbed by them. The teacher's manner toward the group was unaffected by the lack of co-operation of the one or two who had not yet learned to work with the others. In this latter case the teacher's disregard of disturbance was reflected in a similar tendency in pupils. Without conscious effort on the part of the teacher her own calmness and unruffled demeanor seemed to pervade the general classroom atmosphere.

A significant finding that grew out of the analysis of the observations made was that good teachers were distinguishable from poor teachers through the following:

The good teachers were free from the restricting inhibitions and restraints common to the poor teachers. They sought ways to improve their teaching and were open-minded and desirous of suggestion. The poor teachers defended their shortcomings whether called upon or not to do so and called attention to that which they thought would lead to commendation.

In contrast to the ineffective teachers who resorted to threats and to loud, dominating demands, the superior teachers guided children by quiet, humorous, and sometimes inaudible suggestions. Enthusiasm and spontaneity were found to be prevalent in the rooms of the good teachers. In the classrooms of the less successful teachers, nagging, apathy, and a complete absence of zestful enterprise prevailed.

The better teachers treated their pupils with a respectful interest in them as persons. Pupils in the other classrooms did not stand out as individuals except when violating some rule for which they were corrected. There were a friendliness and courtesy in the classrooms of the good teachers but there was a disregarding of personality as such in the classrooms of the tense and striving poor teachers. Teachers and pupils showed a co-operative interest in the undertakings in the classrooms of the better teachers.

Co-operative purpose and planning were conspicuously lacking in the other classrooms.

The observation and study of the six teachers indicated that there were prevailing teacher-pupil relationships in each classroom which were recognizable and capable of analysis. The procedure gave promise of being a possible way of ascertaining teaching effectiveness and of distinguishing personally desirable teachers from those who should not be teaching impressionable pupils. The number of teachers studied was too limited, however, upon which to generalize. It became apparent that more teachers should be studied before the findings of the study could be accepted with confidence.

In summarizing the observations made in each classroom, incidents which were alike in character had been grouped under captions which were found later to be useful in describing the teacher studied. Extended observation might verify the application of certain of these captions of description to effective teachers and the application of the others to the less effective. The possibility was an intriguing one, and the observations were extended as described in the next chapter to thirty-six additional teachers.

CHAPTER III

SUCCESSFUL AND UNSUCCESSFUL TEACHERS CONTRASTED

The study of six teachers previously described was premised on the one major assumption that a teacher's personal effect upon children can be observed. The findings of the study, built up through careful and unbiased observation, verified the validity of this assumption regarding each teacher and gave ample proof of the direct influence of a teacher's behavior upon the pupils'. Day after day classroom incidents of interacting teacher and pupil behavior were observed and recorded in detail. Records of conversations with teachers and pupils were kept as additional substantiating evidence. Without prejudice or bias an exact transcript of classroom proceedings covering selected days during a four months' period was developed for each classroom situation studied. These recorded findings when analyzed showed conclusively that there were recognizable similarities of conduct on the part of teacher and pupils. There was real resemblance between the teacher's personal conduct and that of her pupils.

Furthermore, there were some differentiating characteristics which distinguished teachers who had proved their ability to stimulate children to socially constructive behavior from those who had proved themselves less successful in this respect. By arranging the samplings of behavior as observed in the six classrooms under appropriate descriptive headings, it was possible to compare the typical behavior of both the teachers and the pupils in the six classrooms. The following contrasting phrases seemed to describe and differentiate the effective and noneffective teachers.

EFFECTIVE TEACHERS	NONEFFECTIVE TEACHERS
Having the ability to remain self-controlled in midst of conflicting demands.	Displaying an inadequacy to classroom demands, easily disturbed.
Poised and efficient in directing several simultaneous activities.	Confused and bothered by interruptions and unforeseen demands.
Habitually quiet, poised, and courteous in relations with children.	Demanding, imposing, impatient in relations with children.
Constructive and encouraging in comments and manner.	Resorting to threats and punishments, sarcastic, cross.
Conversational and friendly in relations with pupils.	Tense, stern, and unfriendly with children.
Original and intriguing in voice and manner.	Voice and manner prosaic and colorless. No time for anything but work.
Possessing a sense of humor.	Serious, too occupied for fun or humor.
Eliciting willing response from children.	Eliciting apathetic, even antagonistic, responses from children.

EFFECTIVE TEACHERS	NONEFFECTIVE TEACHERS
Enthusiastic (although often quietly so) about pupils and teaching.	Harassed, disturbed, unsure, with no interest or enthusiasm.
Participating with interest in pupils' activities.	Always the director of children's activities — never a participant.
Interested in helping pupils to direct their own conduct rather than securing conformity through personal domination.	Asking children to conform to the teacher's way.
Possessing sufficient self-restraint to allow children to work through their own problems.	Imposing directions and requirements upon pupils, oblivious of pupil initiative and resourcefulness.
Intelligently independent of inhibiting restraints of traditional practices.	Impressed with the necessity of pleasing someone else.
Ingenious in utilizing opportunities for teaching.	Unaware of opportunities for vitalizing classroom teaching.
Evidencing a planned but flexible procedure with materials and individual needs anticipated.	Absorbed in controlling the immediate situation — no plan in evidence.
Careful in planning with pupils and in guiding them to successful completion of undertakings.	Expecting children to know what to do and seemingly satisfied if they keep busy.
Skillful in directing pupils to evaluate their own work.	Failing to help pupils set up standards of their own.

EFFECTIVE TEACHERS	NONEFFECTIVE TEACHERS
Aware of children's physical and emotional needs as well as their educational needs.	Unaware of all else except accomplishment of academic work.
Interested in pupils as persons.	Interested only in each child's academic progress.
Alert to the differences in individuals, recognizing abilities and limitations.	Little or no understanding or provision for individual variation or difference.

From the study of the six teachers it became apparent that three of the teachers were able to control their relations with children so that the children's purposes and desires were fostered and their expression encouraged. The other three teachers were incapable or at least did not demonstrate their ability to subordinate their own desires and emotional satisfactions to pupil welfare. Through their behavior and through their conversation the effective teachers registered their satisfactions in the independence of thought and action exhibited by their pupils. The other teachers found it satisfying to dwell on children's exemplified conformity to their own wishes and demands. They were wholly unaware of the learner's need for initiating and carrying through a project to a satisfying conclusion. They did not permit opportunity for children to derive joy from self-discovery. They foreshortened learning through imposing solutions and making deductions before the children had time to find answers for their own questions.

Careful study and interpretation of the differences which separate teachers who stimulate learning from those who partially thwart it indicate that the personal emotional maturity and self-direction of the teacher affect every act. For this reason it is not possible to separate the teacher's personality as such and her skill as an instructor as is suggested by many rating sheets. The teacher's ability to stimulate and guide learning depends upon the facility with which she can identify herself with the learner. This in turn seems to depend upon readiness and willingness to forget self and to rejoice with the learner in his satisfaction at discovering for himself.

Learning has its own attendant emotional response. The thrill of grasping an idea has its own internal reward. Of this the noneffective teachers were wholly unaware. They insisted upon preventing this inner thrill for children by overteaching or hurriedly demanding results before children had time to think. They were insensitive to their pupils' right to their own thoughts and seemed impelled to dictate. It was this insensitivity to the manner in which growth takes place that manifested itself constantly and continuously in their relations with their pupils.

An analysis of the characteristics of the effective teachers will indicate that the skillful teacher is the one who can use his or her personality to give an emotional toning to pupils' learning. Feelings of security and personal worth are strengthened in pupils by a teacher who respects the personality of pupils and acts accordingly. The twenty previously listed attributes of effective teachers describe one who has a sympathetic and understanding outlook upon humanity and one who combines a kindly sincerity and personal integrity with professional skill and knowledge of how others learn.

The differences revealed in the study of the three strong teachers and the three weak teachers were so decided and clearcut in their cleavage that they gave promise of being possible distinguishing characteristics of strong and weak teachers in general. To discover the truth of this hypothesis, it was decided to extend the observational procedure to a larger number of teaching situations. To carry out this venture, the services of two experienced observers were obtained and thirty-six additional teachers were chosen for study. These thirty-six teachers were unselected as to the quality of their teaching. The question to be answered by this extended observation was whether or not the captions of description differentiated good teachers from poor teachers.

Teacher-pupil behavior in the thirty-six classrooms was observed, recorded, and later classified under the descriptive phrases which had been developed through the earlier study of the six teachers. Twenty-one of the thirty-six teachers observed rated as effective teachers with all of their behavior being worthy of classification under the captions describing the three originally studied effective teachers. The remaining fifteen of the thirty-six teachers who were observed rated as non-effective teachers. The samples of their behavior fell under the phrases which described the first-studied three noneffective teachers.

It would not interest the reader to attempt a survey of the complete diary records which were made during the months of observation in the thirty-six classrooms. To indicate the supporting evidence amassed by this extension of the observational procedure, a few samples of the typical behavior of the thirty-six teachers are arranged under the captions which differentiate effective from the less-effective teachers. It should be noted that there was no inconsistency of behavior in relation to these captions. While all effective teachers did not possess all of the positive characteristics, no effective teacher possessed any of the negative characteristics. Teachers 7, 12, 13, 17, 18, 20, 23, 24, 25, 29, 33, 34, 37, 39, and 42 were characterized by several of the negative phrases of description. Space and the reader's patience will not justify a complete listing of the many samples recorded.

DESCRIPTIVE CAPTIONS AND SUPPORTING SAMPLES OF TEACHER BEHAVIOR

HAVING THE ABILITY TO REMAIN SELF-CONTROLLED IN THE MIDST OF CONFLICTING DEMANDS

Sample of Positive Behavior:

Teacher 31. Children in this classroom worked with interest and enthusiasm at their own tasks; were polite to others and considerate but absorbed in what they themselves were doing. The teacher was called away several times, but pupils worked at their own tasks concentratedly. Upon returning to the classroom, the teacher continued her interrupted tasks with no evidence of strain or impatience.

Sample of Negative Behavior:

Teacher 25. Toward the end of the social-studies period the teacher was interrupted by a messenger from another room. Pupils started to whisper. Teacher seemed to lose her poise. "All right, all right," said she several times in an attempt to get pupils' attention. Pupils paid no attention but went on talking. The bell rang in a few minutes and the children dashed out, leaving the teacher vainly shouting directions to them. Teacher was flushed, appeared nervous and distraught.

POISED AND EFFICIENT IN DIRECTING SEVERAL
  SIMULTANEOUS ACTIVITIES

Sample of Positive Behavior:

Teacher 32. Pupils were busily engaged in a number of activities getting ready for a bazaar. Some were making posters, others were constructing a booth, while other individuals were working on toys and articles of varied nature. The teacher went about helping here and there and keeping everyone working. The pupils were quite independent and oblivious of the busy atmosphere. Pupils paid no attention to directions not directed to them, but each concentrated upon what he was doing. The teacher's voice was vibrant, and she seemed to enjoy the bustle of the workroom.

Sample of Negative Behavior:

Teacher 17. Children were busy making tom-toms, constructing a stage, writing a play, and practicing a dance. There was much noise and confusion to which the teacher was contributing by calling loudly from group to group. The children who were not concerned with the directions which were being given stopped their work to listen and several times to argue with the teacher.

HABITUALLY QUIET, POISED, AND COURTEOUS IN RELATIONS WITH CHILDREN

Sample of Positive Behavior:

Teacher 31. Teacher polite and courteous to children. Always looked right at them and spoke directly to them.

Bell rang for recess. Teacher announced that those who wished to stay and listen to the report which two boys were going to give might do so. About half remained. Two boys began a conversation during the report. The teacher quietly called the boys to her, telling them that they were thoughtless of others if they talked while others tried to listen. The boys said that they knew that and decided that they had better go outside.

Sample of Negative Behavior:

Teacher 7.   Children went out to recess with much scolding from the teacher about their not wearing their coats. "Don't you know better? You'll catch your death of cold," said she.

"You'll get a cold and then have to stay home and miss your lesson. Then you'll fail."

"Big girl like you, having to be told. But that is about all I can ever expect from you. You have no sense at all," said the teacher sneeringly.

CONSTRUCTIVE AND ENCOURAGING IN
COMMENTS AND MANNER

Sample of Positive Behavior:

Teacher 8.   The teacher and the children sat in a circle. The teacher gave undivided attention to the children's reading. Some of her remarks were: "Come on, David, you know that big word." "They are helping Mary by giving her time to think out the words. We can always get the word if we think hard."

"John will remember that word because he knew it yesterday. It is the name of the dog we read about in our last story."

"My! You caught the teacher making a mistake. Now don't let me catch you." The children played several games, reading and watching words, very much interested, eager, and ready to recite. Several times during the lesson children who were doing seatwork came up and said, "Mrs. ——, may I do so and so?" She answered them pleasantly, "Good little helpers don't interrupt the teacher. If you have finished, there are many other things you can do. Remember we discussed that this morning."

To a little boy who had lost his jar of paste and had come to the teacher asking for another, she replied kindly, "We are good workmen in this room and do not lose our tools. See whether you can remember where you left it when you were using it last. That is what your father would do, and he is a good workman, I know."

Some of the children at the blackboard were practicing writing their names. The teacher kept her eye on them and encouraged each one to do better or to write his name again. They were interested and worked diligently.

Samples of Negative Behavior:

Teacher 7. After one little boy reading slowly and painfully had read aloud about three lines, the teacher said, "That's an absolute failure. Tell your mother that, if she doesn't send you to school every day, you will never get out of the first grade." (Boy looked puzzled and hurt.) Some of the others snickered.

The teacher kept going around and around the circle of chairs, putting children's fingers on words and saying in loud voice, "Why can't you pay attention. You will never learn to read. I've told you ten times today to pay attention. You will fail if you don't do better."

(Children at seats moved around noisily.) The teacher had a snapper in her hand and kept snapping at the children, saying, "Sit down! No talking, Jack! No more moving about! For that you stay after school, George!"

"These are the poor readers." (Aside to observer in loud voice) "You should come when the bright ones are having their lesson. Did you ever hear such a poor reader? Listening to this is what the teacher is paid for."

(Children read in loud and unnatural voices.)

Jotting down grades in a book: "You're a smart boy. I'll give you a good mark."

And "That's no good at all. You get a failure."

To a group who were reading she said loudly as she walked around behind them, "Study silently."

Teacher 12. To boys who were rattling pencils and rulers the teacher said listlessly, "David, you are annoying me." "Jack, why do you annoy me so?" These same remarks were repeated again and again to other children who gave no evidence of attention to them.

Teacher 17. Teacher enthusiastic and pleasant but apparently high strung. Children were called upon to explain what they were doing. They were nervous and uncertain in their explanations. If what they said did not please the teacher, she said, "Go back to your place, and I will call upon Mary who can explain it better."

Teacher 29. Oral drill in addition combinations was being conducted by the teacher. Many pupils lacked interest. "You pupils don't seem to know your numbers. Turn to page —— and study." (This in a cross tone.)

"John, you haven't done anything yet. What's the matter with you?"

"I wish you children knew how to work. You do not have any idea of working hard."

"Albert, you have been sitting all

morning and doing nothing. You go sit over there by yourself and see whether you can work."

Teacher 33. "Jack, give the others a chance." This was said again and again to a boy who was enthusiastic in his responses. Each time he tried to answer a question he was given no encouragement. He finally made no attempt to answer, busied himself with a book, and gave no attention to the discussion.

CONVERSATIONAL AND FRIENDLY IN RELATIONS WITH PUPILS

Samples of Positive Behavior:

Teacher 19. Children spoke in a friendly natural way to the teacher, and the teacher played and joked with them. No child took any advantage or showed undue familiarity.

Teacher 27. Teacher pleasant and gracious to the observer. Children eager to show visitor around the room. Children and teacher were mutually interested in everything in the classroom and chatted with the observer, explaining the unit of work completed, drawings, models, charts, etc.

Teacher 38. The pupils had a discussion period presided over by one of their number. The teacher sat in one of the seats with the pupils. She gave them full rein and only occasionally made a statement and then awaited her turn. Throughout there was a friendly spirit. When they laughed, she laughed with them.

Samples of Negative Behavior:

Teacher 13. Children were at the board working subtraction examples. Each child was called upon to give a step-by-step recital of his problem. Before each child recited, the teacher said, "Step to one side. How do you expect me to see through you?" This was said to fifteen different children.

Teacher 20. Teacher's voice strained and harsh; manner sober; dressed in black. Children listless and without seeming interest or expectancy; more interested in one another than the teacher. The teacher seemed to have no place in their attention.

ORIGINAL AND INTRIGUING IN VOICE AND MANNER

Samples of Positive Behavior:

Teacher 9. Smiling to children, "How would you like to take a trip with me?" Children were expectant immediately. Their faces showed pleasure. Seemingly they knew something pleasant was in store for them.

Teacher 31. Teacher was businesslike but pleasant. Voice quiet but decisive. Pupils were alert and eager to get arithmetic answers. The teacher's quick decisive manner seemed to stir the pupils' physical alertness. Pupils smiled and seemed pleased to be complimented on correct answers. The teacher's manner was intriguing to them.

Sample of Negative Behavior:

Teacher 37. Teacher's manner was not positive. During the hygiene lesson, she asked several questions in a listless, colorless manner. The children stood to answer, but seemed dazed and uncertain of what the teacher had asked. She answered her own questions by reading long, medical terms.

The teacher's desk was far away from the children's, and she seemed far away in interest and spirit from the children. There was no spark of interest aroused.

ELICITING WILLING RESPONSE FROM CHILDREN

Samples of Positive Behavior:

Teacher 16. Teacher was pleasant, was colorfully dressed, and had a soft voice, pretty smile, and genuine enthusiasm. The children were at work upon a variety of projects which they eagerly explained to the observer.

During the music lesson children and teacher sang together songs which they greatly enjoyed. All the boys sang with zest.

Teacher 26.   Pupils and teacher were discussing their excursion to a near-by park. The pupils were telling the teacher about what they had seen, laughing and asking her whether she saw this, that, and the other thing. The teacher, seemingly enjoying their enthusiasm, was urging them to talk. Children were enthusiastic and friendly in sharing with the teacher all that had been seen.

Samples of Negative Behavior:

Teacher 20.   "Come, now, get ready to go," said the teacher. A few straightened up, but most of the children paid no attention whatsoever. The teacher's requests secured little response until she fairly screamed.

Teacher 23.   The teacher's voice was quite soft, lacking animation and tone variation as she presented Roman numerals. The pupils were seemingly uninterested. Some were gazing out of the windows; others were amusing themselves by drawing. One pupil crumpled his drawing, took a sheet of paper, and started to draw again while the teacher continued on without noticing him.

Teacher 33.   The teacher wanted the pupils to write a motto for a certain phase of the project and told them to do so before beginning their free reading. Almost everyone went to get a book and started to read immediately. The teacher reminded them at least three times in a listless, apathetic tone. Not more than a third responded during the entire period.

Pupils were told to put their tools and work away and to get ready for writing of paragraphs. It took ten minutes or more for all to respond to the teacher's request.

Teacher 39. Teacher said, "I want you to leave the room quietly and with all in order when you go."

The bell rang for recess. The children closed their books with a bang and went running out. Desks were not in order, and the floor was littered with papers.

ENTHUSIASTIC (ALTHOUGH OFTEN QUIETLY SO) ABOUT PUPILS AND TEACHING

Samples of Positive Behavior:

Teacher 9. "I love to teach. Only those who enjoy children should be teachers."

Teacher 14. Teacher's comments to observer, "I love to teach. I always have. I love each boy and girl, and I like to see the light dawn on their faces. If I see they are getting discouraged, I give them an easy problem to give them confidence." Several children's comments to observer after school, "We like arithmetic now. Miss —— makes it so easy. We never liked arithmetic until we got in Miss ——'s room.

Teacher 35. Teacher and children, low first graders, sang together with apparent joy. Both teacher and children recalled songs that they could sing and took real pleasure in singing them.

Teacher seemed to make a game of everything. Children were happy and smiling, always ready to play with her.

Samples of Negative Behavior:

Teacher 34. Teacher said that she could not understand how anyone could be interested in visiting schools.

"Sorry to be so uninteresting, but I have other things to do. I always get my clerical work done in school. I am making out report cards. Children don't learn much in school anyway; so what difference does it make whether I teach or make out reports?"

PARTICIPATING WITH INTEREST IN
   CHILDREN'S ACTIVITIES

Samples of Positive Behavior:

Teacher 9. During social-studies lesson, an "Information, Please" program was suggested by a boy. His suggestion was met with general approval by the class. The children asked intelligent questions.

Teacher and pupils entered eagerly and enthusiastically into the game. Teacher seemed as much pleased as did the children when clever and original questions were asked.

Teacher 36. The class was having the usual reading lesson, but the most noticeable thing was the way the teacher entered into the spirit of the story. She was full of fun and enthusiasm, asking all kinds of questions in the most playful manner. The children responded to her playful spirit. They were entirely free from self-consciousness and entered into the game whole-heartedly.

Samples of Negative Behavior:

Teacher 20. This teacher did not seem to know how to enter into children's interests. They seemed to disregard her entirely. She was more interested in getting things done than in what the children did.

"You are big boys and girls and should get things done without noise."

"I would like to see you in your seats all the time."

"Sitting up straight is more important than anything else."

Remarks like these were made continuously, but the pupils paid little attention. They talked to one another, disregarding the teacher who stood helplessly by.

Samples of Positive Behavior:

Teacher 11. The teacher was guiding children in solving arithmetic problems, helping each pupil to work out his own solution. She talked calmly and quietly with the children but was persistent in guiding each so that he knew what to do. After assuring herself that the pupil understood the problem, the teacher made it his responsibility to find the answer and prove it.

During the art period the children talked with each other about their pictures, getting suggestions for colors to use. Not once did the teacher try to impose her wishes on any child. When a child knew what color he wanted to use, the teacher helped him carry out his own idea.

Teacher 14. Children wanted to show observer their play. The teacher became a listener while the children presented the play. The teacher said that the children had written the play, chosen the actors, and rehearsed it entirely by themselves. She believed in such projects, she said.

Teacher 16. In talking with the observer, this teacher said, "I sometimes almost bite my tongue in my effort not to interfere with children's work. I think the children and their activities are most important, and that the teacher should be in the background as a guide rather than a director."

Teacher 21. Teacher discussed with children what might be included in their paintings. She reminded them of the various things seen on the farm, the size relations of animals, house, barn, fences, etc. Some children started to ask a number of questions. The teacher said quietly but firmly, "Now you do your own thinking. Each person must solve his own problems. Each wants to do his own painting and not have it the teacher's thinking or the teacher's work.

Teacher 28. Pupils conducted an assembly program; read poems, stories, sang songs, and played instruments while the teacher was an interested onlooker.

Teacher 38. Teacher sat in one corner of the room. She did not call on the boys and girls. They waited their turns and stood up and voiced their opinions. They often referred to statements made by other students and gave reasons for questioning or correcting their statements. They spoke with assurance and without hesitation.

Samples of Negative Behavior:

Teacher 13. Children were sitting in their seats with poetry books open on their desks reading poems in unison. Poem after poem was read without any break between poems or any comment from the teacher. To one boy who knew the poems and was dramatizing them, the teacher said, "Pay attention to your book and stop acting silly." To another boy who asked a question about a poem, the teacher said, "Do as I say and stop asking me foolish questions." The children were permitted no choice of poems.

Teacher 17. The children were working but came to the teacher constantly to make decisions for them. She was inclined to say, "Make it larger." "Do it this way." "That's not right." It was evident that they were doing things for the teacher and not for themselves or the group.

Teacher 24. Pupils were interested in comparing their workbook answers as they stood around the teacher's desk. "This is my business," said the teacher. "Your business is to do exactly what I tell you and nothing else."

Teacher 29. "Will you never mind how you have been taught to rule your papers. You do it the way *I* want you to do it," said the teacher.

Teacher 33. The teacher led the discussion and accepted or rejected pupils' ideas as she pleased. Pupils volunteered little, seeming to know that the teacher did not want their ideas, but wanted someone to tell her what she had in mind. For the most part the pupils sat and looked.

POSSESSING SUFFICIENT SELF-RESTRAINT TO ALLOW CHILDREN TO WORK THROUGH THEIR OWN PROBLEMS

Samples of Positive Behavior:

Teacher 31. A boy came up to the teacher's desk and asked if he might take a spelling make-up test. The teacher told him to find someone to help him, giving him the list of words. The teacher explained that children could take make-up tests if they asked for them. Otherwise absent time went unaccounted for.

A class meeting was held at the beginning of each day to consider all matters of conduct of the previous day.

The teacher treated pupils in a very direct adult way, expecting them to be individually responsible for themselves.

Teacher 38. Pupils were seated around a table ready to give current events when the teacher entered the room. They had some difficulty among themselves as to how they would start. She busied herself with other things until they told her they were ready to begin.

Samples of Negative Behavior:

Teacher 17. "You are too slow. Let me do it for you. We just must get this work done.

I will have to do it myself after school
if you are so slow."

Teacher 18. The teacher talked most of the time.
She showed children how to use ges-
tures to accompany their poems. Some
children tried to follow their own ideas
as to what was appropriate. To this the
teacher said, "Please follow me exactly.
My way is better."

Intelligently Independent of Inhibiting Restraints of Traditional Practice

Samples of Positive Behavior:

Teacher 16. "I always try to have each child find
his own solutions to problems. All are
different. What works for one is sometimes not understood by another."
Teacher to class, "Try your own way
of doing it. There is no right way that
we all have to follow. Each person
should want to discover a better way
for himself.

Teacher 31. Teacher was conducting a series of ex-
periments to find out whether there
was any correlation between the quality and quantity of the work accomplished with and without music. The
radio was tuned into a program of
classical music while children worked
on arithmetic.
They worked concentratedly, without
any interruptions, for fifteen minutes.
(Children thought they could work better with music.)

Children had visited the Fair and had come back with a list of projects they had been inspired to undertake. The teacher explained that she was willing to have them choose their own projects provided they were of sufficient interest to cause them to utilize their initiative and carry them through to completion.

Teacher 38. The chairman called the meeting to order. Several pupils gave reports. Suggestions and criticisms were requested. One boy stated that two reports did not seem to agree and asked which was correct. The teacher was asked how the pupils might be helped to judge which report was accurate. She explained how foolish it was to guess, but explained that one should have facts before making a judgment and be open-minded to truth. She said that she was always willing to change if a better way could be found but she wanted facts.

A little later a girl made this statement, "That is still in an experimental stage. We should wait for facts."

Samples of Negative Behavior:

Teacher 29. "Children, I have learned how this is to be done. You don't know. Do it just as I tell you and do not ask questions."
To observer: "I never change my way of doing things. Time and effort are saved by using one method. I have no

use for this idea of experimenting. The old way is good enough for me."

Teacher 34. Teacher said that she was sorry to have such an uninteresting lesson but that the lesson was a required one. She thought that she might vary it a bit, but after all, "What is the use of trying anything different. These pupils will never learn anything anyway."

Teacher 12. During arithmetic period pupils became restless and uninterested. Teacher made no attempt to present the arithmetic problems in an interesting way. One child was called upon to work out a problem. The other children paid little attention to these recitations. During the lesson the teacher made these remarks: "Don't do that!" "Pay attention!" "Sit down and listen!" "Turn around!" "I am waiting for you!" "You just want to attract attention!"

During class meeting which was presided over by a pupil, the teacher allowed pupils to criticize one another. The pupil leader was unable to direct the discussion. The teacher did nothing but remind pupils that the meeting should not be a conversation between the speakers and herself.

During news reports several boys who had been uninterested previously now wanted to make reports on various phases of aviation. They asked several intelligent questions, but the teacher's remarks were, "We won't go into that now."

INGENIOUS IN UTILIZING OPPORTUNITIES FOR TEACHING

Samples of Positive Behavior:

Teacher 14. "You know being present is part of our job. Absence is no excuse. What can we do to take care of our absences?" Before they finished, the class had worked out a regular plan for making up absence. One boy was put in charge of the record keeping for a week with others chosen for following weeks.
The teacher said afterward that whenever an important learning situation arose, she made it her plan to use it then and there.

Teacher 15. Quite unexpectedly a child asked why the sun was not shining. The teacher explained what fog was and how the fog kept the sunshine from the earth. "How would you like to start a weather calendar tomorrow? We could keep a record of each day's weather and find out more about weather." The children responded with clapping of hands and smiles.

Teacher 36. The children recited poems and told stories for the visitor. They used a play microphone and announced each number before giving it. (The teacher said that the children took more interest when they played that they were broadcasting.)

The teacher broadcast a new song which she wanted the children to learn, giving the children a fine example of good singing.

EVIDENCING A PLANNED BUT FLEXIBLE PROCEDURE
WITH MATERIALS AND INDIVIDUAL NEEDS ANTICIPATED

Samples of Positive Behavior:

Teacher 8.   When the reading lesson was over, the teacher had the children bring their chairs and make a circle. Then followed a discussion of what they were going to do during the free work period when they came back from lunch. The teacher listened to the children's plans, suggesting ways and means of carrying them out, but did not impose her own ideas. The manner in which the children entered into the discussion indicated that such planning was not new to them but was the usual procedure in the classroom.

Teacher 10.   One half of group doing seatwork. Every child busy and interested. Seemed to know exactly what to do and how to do it. Never once did a child go to the teacher to ask a question. The teacher went around and checked each child's seatwork, praising each for his neatness. When the seat-work was completed, the pupils took out library books or completed some unfinished work which they had in their desks.

Teacher 15. Children were working in two groups; one group was reading while the other group worked on games. The group working on games did not interrupt the teacher but knew exactly what to do. When the reading group finished, a little boy went to the back of the room and brought forward to the teacher a box of games. The children were asked whether they had questions. A few questions were asked. The children then took their seats and with apparent enjoyment began to use their game materials.

At a quiet word from the teacher the next group of children took their chairs to the front of the room and formed a semicircle. Two boys passed out the books, opening one for the teacher and one for the observer. Upon completion of the reading, the teacher asked the pupils to study ahead while she checked the game work of the other group. Pupils studied and as they finished took their chairs to their respective places and individually left the room.

Teacher 21. Pupils took out painting materials and began the lesson, seemingly knowing just what they were to do and how to go about doing it. After a half-hour of work the teacher said, "We have just two minutes to clean pans and to get desks ready." Wet paintings were placed on one side of the desk, brushes were dipped and dried while monitors passed containers into which paint water was emptied. Again every child seemed to know exactly what to do and seemed pleased to do it.

Teacher 31. Children were grouped according to their reading ability and sat in such a way that light came over left shoulders; not in regular straight rows. Children moved about freely, completing one undertaking and then another. They seemed to know just what to do next and where to find materials.

(The classroom had much children's work in it: charts, several large paintings which were well mounted, a wellstocked library which was very much used. The whole classroom indicated that children used everything in it but had been taught to carry out their work according to plan and a previouslythought-through procedure.)

Samples of Negative Behavior:

Teacher 7. Teacher sat down at one of the tables saying, "Bring me your seatwork." Children all came running. knocking over chairs, shouting, "See mine, Mrs. ———."

Then followed such comments by the teacher as these: "You didn't read directions." "You copied from William." "You're no good with colors."

"When are you ever going to do what you are told?"

Children who had perfect papers were given candy at the close of the lesson.

Teacher 17. Classroom was untidy-looking. A number of old clay models had been left until melted and had become grotesque-looking. The worktable was littered with odds and ends. The teacher's desk was in disorder as were the children's desks. Children did not know where to find materials and frequently asked the teacher for articles about whose location the teacher was uncertain.

Teacher 34. Teacher called upon pupils, one by one and row after row, so that pupils felt no need for giving attention. Each read, mumblingly, a half-page or so. Meanwhile, the teacher behind a pile of books and papers was making out report cards. She did not even follow but just said "Next" when she wanted another to read. No attempt was made to explain meanings, correct mispronounced words, or even to notice that at times the pupils left out whole paragraphs. They knew that the teacher was not listening; so they did other things, reading at random when called upon.

CAREFUL IN PLANNING WITH PUPILS AND IN GUIDING THEM TO SUCCESSFUL COMPLETION OF UNDERTAKINGS

Samples of Positive Behavior:

Teacher 15. Three children in the classroom were immature and unable to do the work which other children did. The teacher was patient with these children, always taking time to see that they understood directions. She frequently went over to a child and planned with him individually. The teacher stated that she always took time to see that each child was working under conditions which made him self-sufficient, able to carry on his work without disturbing others, and to complete all the work of which he was capable.

Teacher 19. Children moved their chairs about without confusion or noise. In sitting at their tables, children took time to place the front edge of the chair a uniform distance from the edge of the table. It was evident that children had been taught how to handle their chairs. When leaving the room, children went out in an informal way but keeping to the right and carefully waiting turns. (This practice seemed natural but had been acquired through frequent repetition over a period of time. Teacher said that the children and she had worked out the plan together.)

Teacher 36. The teacher planned with the group of children as to what they would do while the others read. Each child told the teacher what he intended to do. During the time the others read, these children painted, read library books, and worked on things which they were making for the miniature town. At the completion of the reading lesson, the teacher asked each child to tell what he had accomplished in the time at his disposal.

Samples of Negative Behavior:

Teacher 12. At the close of the arithmetic period papers were collected by monitors. There was much confusion with remarks such as these:

"Miss ——, Jack won't give me his paper."

"Miss ——, Mary hasn't finished yet."

"You always get to collect the papers."

The teacher allowed such comments to go on without making any constructive suggestions. It was apparent that there had been no routine planning in this classroom.

Later, when children were dismissed for recess, they were told to get into line. Few did so. Most of the children talked loudly and boisterously, paying no attention to the teacher, who looked on apathetically.

Teacher 33. The girls were asked whether they would work on some sewing for the class project. They took out their work reluctantly for a few minutes. Soon it was put aside, and the girls were visiting with each other. For twenty minutes or more this went on without a word from the teacher who apparently forgot what she had asked the girls to do. No question was raised at the close of the period regarding accomplishment. The unfinished work was shoved into a basket.

The boys in the class worked boisterously and carelessly. Much material was wasted and thrown aside. Little was completed.

SKILLFUL IN GUIDING PUPILS TO EVALUATE THEIR OWN WORK

Samples of Positive Behavior:

Teacher 16. Two little girls explained in great detail the classroom organization, how spelling and arithmetic were checked and how the various diagnostic charts were used.

Following recess, pupils held their criticism period. A child from each row reported what the row had accomplished during the preceding work period and told what the row intended to do next day and what materials were needed.

Criticisms and suggestions for improvement were offered by all. When the pupils had finished, the chairman called on the teacher for her criticisms. From her notes she cleverly tied the suggestions together and helped them on to the next step without saying what she wished them to do.

Teacher 32. A group of five pupils, one of whom acted as chairman, were reporting information needed by all members of the class. Many pictures and charts were used. (The teacher explained that she had supplied references but that pupils had done all their own organizing.) While reporting, the speakers occasionally let their voices get too low to be heard. The teacher waited until one speaker had finished and said, "There is no use taking time to talk if you do not make others hear. What is reporting for?"

As pupils digressed, the chairman commented, "That is interesting, but we were discussing something else. After several speakers had made their contributions, the teacher spoke, comparing conversation to a river with many tributaries. "Each tributary is important, but it is the leader's responsibility to keep the main body of water flowing to the ocean," said the teacher. Later the pupil leader reminded a speaker that it would be better to re-member the main river and not add so many tributaries. The leader asked the members of the class to keep track of the number of tributary ideas that each speaker advanced.

Samples of Negative Behavior:

Teacher 20. Children made error after error and smiled about their mistakes. Those who did poorly seemed as well satisfied as those who were perfect. Nothing was said about results.

As in the arithmetic lesson, the children read carelessly and without effort. The teacher accepted the poor work as readily as the good. She offered no suggestions to the children which would help them judge their own work or cause them to improve.

Teacher 39. From time to time the teacher tried to have pupils correct their own grammar. They laughed outright and paid no attention to corrections.

AWARE OF CHILDREN'S PHYSICAL AND EMOTIONAL NEEDS
AS WELL AS THEIR EDUCATIONAL NEEDS

Samples of Positive Behavior:

Teacher 32. Teacher knew home backgrounds from which the children came. She planned her work to challenge their abilities, she said. She placed them in positions where leadership would be required. Most of the class activities, according to the teacher, involved activities which permitted pupils to make individual contributions. Her purpose of organizing in this manner was to provide each with experiences for enjoying the results of both giving and sharing. Always the teacher kept in mind, she said, that the school needed to supplement the home.

Teacher 35. This teacher had visited in the homes of all her pupils and knew the parents of the children. She said that knowing the home environment helped her to understand the pupils. The truth of this was evidenced in the little personal comments which she made to pupils and which caused them to smile in a friendly and understanding way and do just what the teacher suggested.

Samples of Negative Behavior:

Teacher 18. Only girls recited. Boys were not called upon and seemed uninterested and bored. (The poems the girls recited were about dolls and pretty dresses. There were no boys' poems.)

ALERT TO THE DIFFERENCES IN INDIVIDUALS, RECOGNIZING ABILITIES AND LIMITATIONS

Samples of Positive Behavior:

Teacher 16. During the arithmetic lesson some pupils went to the board while others worked at their seats. The teacher went about helping each child individually.

As pupils finished, they went to work on their projects. The teacher gave her entire attention to those having difficulty. She knew exactly what each pupil needed and how much of the work he could grasp.

Teacher 41. Two of the boys who found it hardest to adjust were asked to show the observer around the room. The teacher said before the boys that they were trying to be so helpful and she knew they would be nice to a visitor. The boys were careful to point out everything and seemed pleased to be given the special honor.

This teacher knew how to encourage each individual and to suggest his practicing that which he needed most. She smiled and encouraged but quietly insisted upon each trying what she thought he needed to try.

Samples of Negative Behavior:

Teacher 7. No allowance was made for slow pupils. Slow pupils had to see the bright ones given candy. Their faces showed their disappointment. To make it harder, the teacher said, "You slow children will never get any candy, I guess."

Teacher 42. The children were asking questions prepared from the text. The lesson was a routine affair to which all were quite indifferent. The teacher did not enter into the discussion at all.

The teacher said that teaching slow children was "horribly dull." "It takes so long for everyone to learn the lesson that it is a continuously dull process," said she. No provision whatsoever was made for individual differences of pupils.

Teacher 33. Boys responded eagerly to questions asked by the teacher. Girls were apathetic and had to be addressed twice before they responded. The subject matter pertained to inventors, and activities centered about this theme. The girls were uninterested, and the teacher did nothing to find opportunities for the girls which would appeal to them.

INTERESTED IN PUPILS AS PERSONS

Samples of Positive Behavior:

Teacher 9. Remarks to observer: "I want pupils in my room to be interested in adjusting to members of their own social group rather than in doing good work just to please me. I try to learn as much as I can about the home and background of each child. Each child has many of his own problems to face and solve."

Teacher 40. Children were making up arithmetic problems. Someone made a problem involving the number of children in his family. This led later to a discussion of how brothers and sisters could help each other and mother and father. The teacher was kindly and interested in all they had to say. She encouraged their talking in order to learn more about their home conditions so that she might know "their environmental needs," as she later told the observer.

Samples of Negative Behavior:

Teacher 12. "You act as if you had not had any home training. What is your home like anyway?" The teacher seemed serious in asking this question and waited for the boy to answer. The child became embarrassed, and his face flushed. All the other pupils stared at him.

"I wish I had time to visit your homes. I might know more about you if I did."

Teacher 39. "These children come from dreadful homes. I have to treat them as I do or they would run over me. All I can do is to keep them busy and shout them down. They don't appreciate anything else."

In summarizing the behavior of the teachers who contribute to the full and rounded development of children, it should be said that above all else they were capable of effecting a natural person-to-person relationship between themselves and their pupils. They discovered pupils' abilities and capitalized upon them. Through careful planning they guided pupils into activities in which they could successfully make a contribution to the group of which they were members. By so doing, they encouraged diffident children to try and confident ones to encounter challenging tasks. These teachers showed genuine interest in pupils and in their undertakings, even to the extent of entering wholeheartedly with them into their games, in-school activities, and out-of-school hobbies. They treated pupils with respect, asking their opinions and giving them their own, not in a condescending or patronizing manner, but with directness and with convincing honesty. Each one of the good teachers possessed some intriguing manner of speech or action which seemed to make children want to listen. All were poised individuals and were able to face conflicting demands without becoming hurried or petulant with their pupils.

Although direct attention was not given to methods and teaching techniques employed by teachers, there was an evident ability to plan and execute plans with dispatch and resourcefulness on the part of the good teachers. They were independent in their thinking and were inclined to use only those suggestions within a course of study or prearranged program which they thought appropriate for their classes. They exercised judgment in what to teach and when to teach it and could give supporting reasons for their decisions. In guiding pupil activities, they were unhurried. They were concerned more with providing opportunities for extending the experience of their pupils than in realizing immediate academic learning. They did not seem to be actuated by the necessity of having their pupils accomplish a given amount of work within the shortest possible time, but were leisurely and relaxed in their guidance. All of these effective teachers seemed actuated by a desire to have children assume responsibility for themselves. Their guiding philosophy, as expressed by many of them, was to have their pupils form such habits of thought and of work as would be foundational to satisfying and useful living.

An analysis of the effectiveness of teachers would be wholly incomplete without consideration of the apparent reactions of pupils. While the samples of teacher behavior included in this chapter necessarily have included evidences of pupil response, direct attention has not been given to pupils in the classrooms studied. In the chapter immediately following, an attempt will be made to evaluate pupil behavior in classrooms presided over by teachers of contrasting effectiveness. While it has been impossible to control all conditions affecting pupils' classroom behavior other than the effect of the teacher, only children's behavior within the same school will be compared. By keeping the comparison within the same school conditions, environmental factors will be held somewhat constant.

CHAPTER IV

DESIRABLE PUPIL BEHAVIOR

Every classroom has an atmosphere created by the interaction of personalities which is either conducive or detrimental to the best all-around development of children. Since behavior is learned, the manner in which the child learns to conduct himself in the class-room contributes directly to his total behavior as a person. In school pupils acquire not only habits of work and study but also ways of reacting to others. They form attitudes about themselves and about others which are basic to subsequent living. Too often not enough attention is given to this phase of learning. Educators are aware of it, but insufficient time is taken to make critical analyses of just what habits pupils in contact with particular teacher personalities are acquiring. It is the purpose of this chapter to lift to a place of attention the observable behavior of pupils as seen in the classrooms of some of the teachers described in the previous chapter. An attempt will be made to analyze and to evaluate this behavior in terms of the needs of growing children as previously outlined.

Those needs, as it will be recalled, are of a triple nature: needs which pertain to the fulfillment of cer-

75

tain physical urges having to do with bodily requirements for food, rest, physical exercise and relaxation,
the determiners of the physiological tempo of the body;
needs which center in the individual's desire for social
recognition and approval; and needs which arise from
the individual's growing concern for his own worth as
a person. It will be recognized that this categorical arrangement of needs is one for convenience only. Behavior being complex, outward manifestations cannot
be attributed to inner causes with any degree of certainty or of accuracy. It seems obvious, however, even
to the more casual student of behavior who studies his
own inclinations that all three of these grouped needs
demand satisfaction. Situations which deprive individuals, particularly immature and growing individuals,
of the natural satisfactions which inherent needs require may cause substitute fulfillments to be sought.
Normal and healthy habits are dependent upon free
and unhampered satisfying of the legitimate psychological and physiological needs of life, particularly in
the early years in which habits are being formed. If
teachers are unaware of these needs, they frequently
are responsible for children's seeking satisfaction
through undesirable habits of expression.

The opportunities for normal growth afforded some
children and denied others within the same school
can be attributed directly to the teacher's influence
in the classroom environment. Teacher 19 and Teacher
20, samples of whose behavior are included in the pre-

vious chapter, are examples of adult personalities whose understanding of children's needs and whose influence upon children are in direct contrast. Teacher 19 was a person who was conversational and friendly in her relations with children. She knew their interests and was able to skillfully guide them to successful completion of their undertakings. Her manner was animated; yet she was poised and deliberate. Teacher 20 elicited little response from children. She did not enter into their activities but stood aloof as a drab figure looking on querulously.

The following diary notations depict the details of instruction as carried on in these two classrooms within the same school.

In the classroom of Teacher 20, which was located in a rather dark basement room, the children sat with their backs directly to the windows, with the teacher's desk in front of them. The walls were bare of decorations, and there were no evidences of the pupil's work anywhere to be seen. The teacher was dressed in sober black. Nowhere in the room was there the slightest bit of color except in the little girls' dresses and the boys' shirts.

The teacher spoke in a loud, strained voice to the pupils who showed little animation and interest in what she said. For twenty minutes she talked to the children about the way to form the various capital letters of the alphabet. They squirmed about in their chairs, scraping them noisily on the floor. The teacher continued her instructions, frowning first at one and then at another, using with each interrupting noise a more strident tone of voice.

The children were told to write a sentence which the teacher put on the board. No directions were given about a comfortable position, but the children were admonished to sit still. For thirty minutes the children copied one sentence time after time, the only suggestion from the teacher being that their writing would improve if they sat still. The recess bell finally brought the lesson to a close. The children ran pell-mell from the room, emitting a loud cry of pent-up emotion.

After returning from recess the children were told to take out their books and read. One reading group read aloud to the teacher while the remaining children intermittently read and listened to what was being read. No child was permitted to leave his seat during the entire fifty minutes.

In the classroom of Teacher 19, which was located in a sunny room overlooking a great expanse of rolling hills, the children moved about the room, building barns, silos, troughs, and fences for the classroom farm which was being constructed following a visit to a neighboring farm. The teacher's bright smock made a colorful spot wherever she happened to be seen, working with first one group of children and then with another. There were a few well-mounted pictures of children in action, but for the most part the children's own drawings, clay models, and woodwork adorned the display places in the room.

After the children had been at work hammering, sawing, and fitting parts together for thirty minutes or so, the teacher sounded a low, vibrant chord on the piano and all stood still, quietly awaiting instructions. There followed five minutes of busy clean-up and then the children gathered about the teacher for a story before the bell rang. At the sound of the bell, the teacher and children walked out of the room together.

Following recess, the teacher asked the children to sit in their seats with heads down on their desks while she sang them a new lullaby she wanted them to know. The children's faces, after the brief period of rest and relaxation, had cooled. They and the teacher then discussed what had been accomplished in their morning work period and discussed what they planned to do on the following day. All seemed eager and enthusiastic about their plans. The teacher encouraged each child to tell what he expected to do. Several children said that they could hardly wait for the next day to come.

The children in both of these classrooms were first-grade children, ranging from six to seven years of age. Teacher 19 was aware that children of this age range have a high rate of metabolism, that their energy is expended readily, and that their bodies require alternating activity and rest. This teacher knew that children of this age, because of their physical needs, should not be expected to give attention for more than a half-hour or so to a physically confining task. The children's readiness to comply, the absence of strain and tension, and the eagerness with which they responded testify to this teacher's insight into children's physiological needs. In contrast to children in the classroom of Teacher 20, these pupils were having a natural outlet for their energy. They were using large muscles and were experiencing genuine satisfaction in contributing the results of their own effort to a co-operative project.

The natural inclination to move about was not being permitted children in the classroom of Teacher 20. They were kept busy at tasks of little or no interest to them. Each was allowed no social intercourse with classmates and consequently was learning nothing of the give-and-take of social life. Hampered physically, restrained socially, given no opportunity for personal expression, it is no wonder that these children had to be coerced. It takes no imagination to surmise that these children were learning to think of school as a place of disagreeable tasks and of the teacher as a taskmaster who was to be disregarded if possible. None of the needs of childhood were being met in this classroom in so far as observation permitted a judgment to be made. The physical, mental, and emotional aspects of growth seemingly were unknown to this teacher who had to demand attention. Children were not learning to think and act for themselves but to submit to direction which was obviously uninspiring. They were not experiencing the joy of zestful accomplishment.

The classroom atmosphere of two contrasting sixth-grade situations within the same school is well pictured by selecting a few of the recorded observations made in the two rooms. As in the first-grade classes, it will be obvious that pupils in one classroom are enjoying opportunities for personal growth and development which are not afforded pupils in the other room. Teacher 16 and Teacher 18, the two teachers of these sixth-grade classes, are described briefly but with sufficient clarity to suggest the influence of their respective personalities upon the pupils for whose development they are responsible.

Teacher 18 was a rather expressionless person who, though pleasant, was serious about her work. Her voice was weak, and she was inclined to be quite dramatic in her actions.

The pupils sat in formally arranged desks and seats, appearing rather listless and apathetic about what was going on.

During the arithmetic lesson which consisted of four problems involving the adding of mixed numbers, the teacher sat at her desk correcting papers. When all had completed the problems, individual pupils were called on for correct answers. If an incorrect answer was given, another pupil was asked for the answer. Without explanation, children were required to indicate their correct answers and pass their papers in. The lesson for the next day was then assigned.

A command for "Stand! Step into the aisle and follow me," was given to the children, who mechanically arose and imitated the teacher's bending and breathing exercises.

In preparation for an assembly program, the teacher announced a practice period to be devoted to the recitation of poems. The girls responded with evident feeling and expression. As suggested by the teacher, they used their hands to supplement the words. The boys stood and went through the motions most reluctantly. They gazed off into space as if to avoid the eyes of each other. There was apparent disgust in their faces.

During the audience reading period which followed, pupils were asked to come to the front of the room to read. The others sat with their books open. There were no questions asked nor any discussion encouraged. Most of the pupils did not read loud enough for those in the back of the room to hear. Several lost their opportunities to read because they did not know the place.

Toward the close of the afternoon the children were told to take out their assignment books and copy the assignments for next day. These assignments included pages to be read at home and pages to be read in school on the day following.

The teacher then requested that desks and floor be cleaned, accompanied the children to the door and then returned "to pick up the pieces and try to forget that tomorrow would be another day of the same thing."

Teacher 16 was a small, colorfully dressed woman, pleasant in manner, with a soft voice, radiant smile, and apparent enthusiasm.

The pupils sat at tables on one side of the room. On the other side was a long worktable which was covered with partially finished objects of construction. Maps, pictures, and children's work hung on the walls. After a little informal test for comprehension of some reading which had been completed, pupils took out their arithmetic books and began working.

Each pupil seemed to be working on problems of his own choice. The teacher moved about, sitting first with one and then another, helping and testing each. As the recess bell rang, the teacher left the pupils to dismiss themselves and explained to the observer that pupils had been practicing on number combinations which their last diagnostic test had indicated to them they did not know.

Reconvening after recess, the pupils went immediately to work on their various projects, which consisted of a mission, a silver mine, a relief map of Mexico, a Mexican movie, several marionettes, Mexican dolls, booklets on Mexico, individual maps, pictures, and miniatures of Mexican-life scenes.

The children described for the visitor their projects with seriousness and concern. They explained how their work fit into the class activity and the great need for everyone's completing his own "job." All worked busily, some in conference with others, while some applied themselves to their construction without reference to anyone else. When "clean-up time" was announced, chairmen took charge of rounding up their respective committee's materials. Those who finished putting away their materials took seats in the front of the room and awaited the general chairman who directed them in an evaluation and criticism of their own work. Plans were made for the next work period, and the teacher's advice was sought on problems and proposals for the plans of the following day. The teacher, consulting her notebook, made numerous suggestions for improvement.

At the close of school many children lingered to tell the teacher what they were going to do after school. Three different groups were meeting after school to gather materials and make further plans for their marionette show.

Teacher 16 in discussing her teaching expressed an eagerness to visit other schools and to talk with other teachers. She said that her constant challenge was to find opportunities for capable children to initiate and at the same time to provide sufficient repetition and practice for the children who learn less rapidly. This teacher was concerned with pupils who want to start many things and complete none. She said that she had found that the pressure of the group was the best antidote for this. The daily evaluation period was a stimulus to the less diligent.

Pupils in the classroom of Teacher 16 were learning to assume responsibility for directing their own work and for evaluating its usefulness. They were experiencing the demands of co-operative endeavor. Like the younger pupils in the class of Teacher 19 they were spending their hours in school on tasks which were of their own selection and were of worth to them. They were having the guidance of a thoughtful teacher in carrying through to successful completion their undertaken tasks. The joy of accomplishment was not prevented, however, by a dominating adult trying to mold all effort into a pattern outcome. The pupils knew what they were trying to do, had a reason for expending their energy, and were enthusiastic about fitting their individual contributions into the class project.

In the classroom of Teacher 18 self-directing citizenship was not being developed. The teacher was not unsympathetic but possessed neither the insight nor the enthusiasm for helping pupils work out their own plans. Preconceived ideas prevented Teacher 18 from seeing children's interests. Her pupils were assigned lessons and were trying to reach the adult standards which she held with consequent apathy and lack of spontaneity. No provision was made in this room for a socially controlled society. Teacher domination and direction made it impossible for children to learn to organize for the conducting of their own affairs. Individuals were not learning their own strengths and weaknesses through participation, nor were they experiencing the discipline of group control.

Throughout their years in school young people are being molded by both kinds of teachers, those who are alert to their needs and those who are blinded by strict conformity to outmoded procedures. Teachers 38 and 34 are two such teachers. The low tenth-grade English class of Teacher 34 is a good illustration of a teacher's insensitivity to the needs of present-day youth.

Teacher 34 was a middle-aged woman whose whole attire was drab and colorless. Her faded black dress was well spotted with chalk. Her hair was carelessly arranged, and her hands were ink-stained. She was pleasant in manner, but her whole demeanor reflected a weariness of spirit.

The classroom was bare-looking with old faded

copies of pictures of Lincoln, Washington, and Roosevelt pinned high on the front wall. The blackboards were gray with traces of chalk showing. The chairs were in uneven rows, and the teacher's desk was piled high with paper.

To the observer who entered before the class assembled, the teacher was cordial but stated frankly that she couldn't understand anyone's wanting to visit schools. Soon thirty or more boys came in, took their chairs, and sat waiting for the teacher to begin. She immediately passed out papers which were prominently marked with red-ink corrections. With a mere glance most of the pupils crumpled their papers and threw them toward the wastebasket. Many of the crumpled papers failed to reach the basket and were left on the floor. The teacher seemed too busy distributing papers to see what was happening.

The class was asked to give attention to some long sentences which were written in small, fine writing on the blackboard. The teacher said that each contained some slang expression which she wanted them to correct. "Flunked," "exam," "math," "guy," were some of the words pronounced slang by the teacher. The pupils knew no substitutes for these words. One boy expressed the apparent opinion of the class when he said, "Aw, why do we have to learn a lot of new words we don't understand. We know 'em this way. Isn't that enough?" Such reasons as college, business, letter writing, and good English made no appeal. The twelve sentences, however, were corrected during the period. As the bell rang, the boys picked up their books noisily and ran while the teacher protested feebly that she had forgotten to make an assignment for the next day.

On the following day the lesson was called a remedial-reading lesson. Every boy was asked to read aloud which he did in a mumbling way or by trying to read so fast he became wholly confused. While all sat with their books open, no one knew the place when asked to read. Whole paragraphs were skipped without the concern of anyone. The teacher was too busy working on reports to know what was happening. The boys realized that no check was being made and were doing as they pleased, some reading magazines, some story books, another was writing music, and several were looking out of the window. The bell recalled their attention, and again they left the room with the teacher lamenting that she had not found time to make the assignment.

Teacher 38 was an alert-looking, middle-aged woman, well-groomed, and businesslike in manner. Her voice was well-modulated, and her movements were deliberate. She seemed very much at ease, showing no evidence of tension or strain.

The room was sunny and cheerful, with attractive, colorful posters on the side walls. Several well-cared-for maps were on the front wall. The teacher's desk was neat and attractive with flowers and books well arranged.

The observer entered the room after the bell had rung and found pupils sitting around tables, reading magazines and daily papers. As soon as the teacher was seated, a student took his place at the front of the room, calling the class to order. "This is our current-events day," said he, "and I think our first talk is to be on a *Newsweek* article about Germany." One report followed another with much discussion, reference to maps, and occasional use of books to prove debated statements. Throughout the period the chairman presided and kept the discussion to points at issue. When the teacher was invited to participate, she commented on the need for citing authority for statements made and for reserving judgment until facts were known. The effect of her remarks was reflected in the students' talks from then on. Typical of the attention given the teacher's warning was this, "At the present time these seem to be the facts, but we will have to wait before we can say definitely that we know this to be true."

Following the class vote for chairman of the next current-events period, the teacher asked that the groups around the tables take a little time to discuss the subject about which they had been reading, namely, the development of music throughout the ages. Ten minutes or more were given to conversation by students sitting around the several tables. One table was selected as the round table for the day. The students at this table carried on their conversation loudly enough for all to hear, with the listeners knowing that a little later they would be invited to participate. No student was asked to speak, but in natural conversational manner the students, as they wished, entered into the discussion.

When the teacher explained afterward that certain of the modern dances had been banned in the school and that she had selected this way of "letting the students get their pent-up feelings out of their systems," pupils' comments and arguments took on added meaning. Some of their comments were these:

"You do get tired of listening to too much hot music."

"Once in a while a little good classical music is restful."

"Jazz wakes you up. Classical music puts you to sleep."

"Young folks prefer jazz, but, when they get old like their dads, they like operas too."

"Jazz and jitterbug release your energies. They are in tune with the modern age."

"Classical music is used in asylums to quiet the insane."

"When I take my girl to a dance and she has a pretty dress on, I don't think it looks nice to swing her around the way you have to in jitterbug. It's all right for acrobats but not for me."

"Jazz comes from the African jungle. Who wants to imitate those low types?"

"It's only a fad like the 'big apple.'"

"Jazz is nothing more than classical music in a different rhythm."

"In a jazz orchestra, especially a swing one, there is chance for individuality."

During the conversation the teacher sat in one corner of the room. Occasionally she commented. All the correcting of statements and references to "poor grammar" were made by the students. The teacher entered into the spirit of the discussion with real enjoyment. She laughed heartily with the students.

At the close of the conversation the teacher asked for someone to volunteer a summary of the discussion. There were several who responded. They agreed on the general trend of opinion, which was this, "A little hot music is necessary, but you can't stand it all the time; jitterbug is a fad and will die out;

classical music will live, as it appeals to all ages. Civilized people should not imitate the dances of the 'Hottentots.' "

Some of the teacher's own comments are significant. They indicate the purposes underlying the classroom procedure which she encouraged. Said she, "Bright boys and girls like these should have all possible experience for leading. They should learn that knowledge is essential to confidence. I try to have them realize for themselves that their contribution is worth while only if they act with all facts known.

"I do not require class attendance if students have real reason for participating in some other school activity. They have to learn to use their own time. I try to have them make wise choices. However, there is a standard to be met by every member of this class. They know that and choose whether they can afford to be away or not."

As opposed to the lack of opportunity for social growth and critical thinking in the classroom of Teacher 34, students in the classroom of Teacher 38 were learning to discuss problems of vital concern to themselves. They were learning to temper their personal opinions and to seek for facts. These students were acquiring the art of conversation and were able to express themselves with ease and confidence. As indicated by the teacher, they were expected to make decisions for themselves concerning that which they thought of worth to them. Treated as persons whose opinions were respected, they were accorded full responsibility for their own acts and for their opinions as well. The classroom was a place to which they came voluntarily and in which debatable issues were discussed.

While in this classroom there existed a spirit of tolerance, of individual freedom and of social control, there was also an expected performance of high quality. The teacher was alert to the capacities and abilities of her students. She was able to create an environment that had within it demands for accomplishment. Loose, careless thinking and expression were not tolerated. There was an exactness and precision about this teacher which, in spite of her geniality, caused students to respect a high standard of behavior and of accomplishment. Disciplined conduct and real effort were by no means overlooked. Each student was expected to contribute his best. The exchange of opinion followed investigation and study. Lack of preparation and lack of readiness for an attempted discussion were not accepted. The students in this classroom earned their personal freedom.

If pupils in American schools could all have the opportunities for individual development which these better classroom situations offer, a generation of socially intelligent and personally adequate citizens would be in the making. Young children need limitless opportunities for orienting themselves in their physical world. Their bodies need to grow unhampered and unrestricted. Their social horizon needs to be developed and broadened through meeting increasingly involved social demands. Only as they learn to play and work with others will they acquire basic experience for participation in a world of social complexity.

As children mature, they need to learn their own powers and their own weaknesses. Nothing will reveal these to them as effectively as self-discovery. School should provide an experience so broad that every individual can find activities in which he can succeed as well as those in which he proves less efficient. It is not the teacher's place to act as "shock absorber" and to minimize failures for children, but rather to guide them into channels of successful enterprise which will offset other defeats. The child from nine to twelve especially needs to learn to accommodate his thought of himself in a realistic way. With prowess admired at this age level, every child should be helped to gain some legitimate recognitions from his peers.

The adolescent girl and boy need to know themselves and to understand each other. Actuated by urges which are new to them, they require patient guidance and opportunities for adjustment to a world viewed from new perspectives. The school may exert a particular influence at this time when the adolescent is outgrowing standards previously established. Wise counsel and advice given by a respected teacher may tide pupils through troublesome problems at a time when their ideals are being challenged. The school, by furnishing an environment in which adolescent boys and girls may meet each other in wholesome social pursuits, may serve youth at this trying period of their development. Every teacher of adolescents should be a counselor in the true sense.

The present is calling for a "self-disciplined" citizenry. The school will be able to make its greatest contribution to growing citizens if it can provide all children with opportunities for personal and social growth which are comparable to those suggested in the briefly described classrooms of Teachers 19, 16, and 38.

CHAPTER V

AN EFFECTIVE TEACHER DESCRIBED

There probably is not any single configuration of personal attributes which characterizes all effective teachers. This makes it somewhat difficult to describe superior teachers in such manner as to make any one description suggestive to teachers in general. There is no pertinent reason for picturing a teacher in terms of personal physical characteristics, such as color of eyes, facial features, distinguishing idiosyncracies or lack of them. Posture, mode of dress, and many other particulars of interest to one about to employ a certain teacher are not significant terms for general description. While these are of utmost importance in an adequate description of a given individual teacher, they offer no clues to teachers for increasing their own effectiveness.

The description which is to be attempted here is based not upon any adult assumptions about the teaching personality which is effective but upon one highly succeessful teacher's demonstrated influence upon children. The selected teacher inspired the quality of pupil responsiveness and behavior which were outlined in Chapter I of this book as being fundamental to democratic living.

The thought was developed in the first chapter that democracy was a process or way of living with roots grounded in human relationships. The content of the relationships or the impetus which causes the interplay of personalities varies with the purposes of the individuals concerned. Time and place determine the substance of contacts, but the way of working together, if it is democratic, is beyond the confines of time and place. The relationship of individual to individual can be characterized or defined once and for all. It is this significant relationship between the teacher and her pupils that will be specifically illustrated and defined in this chapter. It is the quality of interaction which is worth consideration. The details would vary with each situation. There is no pattern to be offered but an observable and definable interaction that is the enduring factor in true democratic classroom life. It will be recalled that at the outset of the book it was indicated that modern American education if it is to build for democratic living has certain very definite obligations to perform. It has the responsibility of guilding children to respect the rights and privileges of others, to be tolerant of the viewpoints of others, and to take an active part in sharing responsibility for group enterprise and group accomplishment. The classroom was to be thought of as a laboratory in which children, under the wise counsel of the teacher, learned to set up the necessary controls for living together effectively. In the classroom of the teacher about to be presented, control and direction evolved from within the group itself. The teacher was not a dominant force but was instrumental in having children take upon themselves much of the responsibility for the management of their own affairs. Supporting evidence of the teacher's skill in this particular will be offered later.

It was further stressed that pupils needed to be resilient in their adaptability to change. With modern industrial progress and invention causing rapid and sudden improvements in living conditions, pupils in school today need to be alert to possible conditions to be expected in the future. Not only do they need to know and to understand the rapidity with which change occurs but actually to experience adjustment to new situations. Numerous examples will be cited to show how the pupils in the classroom of the chosen teacher, who from this point on will be designated as Miss X, demonstrated the ease with which they became immediately oriented to untried situations which were thoughtfully planned by the teacher.

There were three prominent characteristics discernible in Miss X which seemed to have direct bearing upon her pupils' reactions. While classroom incidents will best illustrate the characteristics, mention is made of these qualities that they may be kept in mind as the specific illustrations of each are cited. First, Miss X displayed few, if any, prejudices of a personal nature which influenced her approach to her own problems or to those of the classroom. In the second place, Miss

X lived a full and a satisfying life outside the school, having many interests and cultural assets. Thirdly, she had a genuine interest in people and in teaching which insured rapport of unusual quality with her pupils. This latter will need careful explanation and illustration that it may be understood, for it in itself is the crux of all attempted definition of good teaching.

The first-mentioned quality of Miss X's, that of open-mindedness or freedom from prejudice and restraint, was illustrated again and again in her relations with her pupils. Incident after incident indicated her deliberate effort to have children arrive at their own decisions without being influenced by her. The consistency with which this characteristic was exhibited gave rise to a question concerning it which brought this direct answer from Miss X concerning the quality which she knew she possessed and which she consciously fostered in herself.

"I have no fixed point of view for my own actions, but, when a problem arises to be settled, I have formed the habit of listening to all the pertinent facts, then weighing the evidence, and in the light of the facts deciding upon what is the best course to take. To make decisions for myself in this way has meant so much to me that I think children should have the same stimulus and satisfaction."

Miss X had learned, she said, that, when the more mature person in association with the children permits those whom he wishes to guide to assume responsibility for their own conduct, the results are generally acceptable to all concerned. She thought that the productive way of securing full and free participation of pupils was to let them have a hand in planning. Consequently, when there was a new undertaking to be launched, the matter was presented to her class as a whole. They were encouraged to discuss what they thought of the project and how they would like to approach it. Negative opinions were solicited as freely as were more positive points of view. Pupils were urged to explore the possibilities within the work before they agreed to undertake it. They appraised the opportunities for original contributions, for enjoyment, and for their own personal growth. No pressure was exerted for an immediate decision. Sufficient time was permitted for full exploration and inventory. When a majority of the pupils were ready to agree to a plan of procedure, discussion was expected to cease and group action begin.

Organization for carrying through to completion a group-accepted task further exemplified Miss X's proclivity to withhold her own opinion. When it came time to organize for work, committee chairmen were chosen by popular vote after their aptitude for the respective responsibilities had been duly considered. Chairmen were free to select their associates but had to give reasons for their choices. Brief rules to govern conduct were set up by all pupils, and with the approval of the committee-of-the-whole each pupil set forth to accomplish a well-defined task which had its place in the group contract. While the teacher's opinion was sought, it was offered with no more intent to influence than that of one of the pupils.

Miss X's own courtesy in offering her opinion seemed to stimulate a like courtesy in pupils. Because she unpatronizingly offered her suggestions to pupils, they reacted with dignity and with an apparent feeling of self-worth. Never was a child put at a disadvantage by having his contribution disregarded or underestimated. If the teacher considered a proposal unworkable, the pupil was guided to the place where he saw its weakness and was helped to salvage it or propose something else. There was an observable carry-over of this same consideration in the pupils' acceptance of one another's ideas.

The habit of listening to others is an acquired one. Miss X thought that it was worth developing in oneself. She not only exemplified the practice of not putting her own convenience first but had a positive effect in helping children to overcome their natural tendencies to be self-centered. Realizing that one of the obligations of "growing up" is to see oneself in relation to others, she was aware of the need for guiding children in this habit. About this, Miss X said:

"While I realize the necessity for both children and adults to make decisions for themselves, I think it is also important for children to adjust to others and to realize that they are adjusting. Awareness of the fact that they are adjusting should prevent a feeling of magnanimity or of self-pity. Children should learn to adjust, to know that they are adjusting, and to realize that it is beneficial to them to be flexible; not flexible to the point of sacrificing personal conviction but to the point of examining personal convictions in light of accepted responsibility to others."

Teachers are often sensitive to the opinion others will form regarding their teaching ability. In attempted self-justification for some traditionally unacceptable classroom conduct on the part of pupils, they feel obliged to explain or justify the conduct. Not so Miss X. A striking example of her willingness to let events speak for themselves occurred in relation to an incident witnessed in the classroom.

Miss X was called out of the room without opportunity to give pupils any suggestions for their work while she was out. For ten or fifteen minutes the pupils continued with the tasks at hand. As these were completed, some boys and girls turned to books and soon were quite absorbed in their reading. A few began to talk and before long, eight or ten had gathered round a table to locate certain places on a large globe. Argument ensued and voices became loud and uncontrolled. Pupils who had previously been occupied were disturbed by the noisy conversation, and three of the girls attempted to have the group of children at the table take their seats. Their attempted control was unavailing. Instead of the noise abating, it was increased by the efforts of the majority to control the few.

This incident took place on a Friday afternoon, and in telling of it the following week, Miss X stated that she had returned to find the class in quite an uproar. She listened to a brief rehearsal of the cause of the disturbance and then suggested that the class might enjoy a music lesson. For the remaining few minutes of the afternoon the pupils sang favorite songs and were dismissed as usual without any comment concerning their inability to "carry on" in the teacher's absence. It was not until Monday that the incident was mentioned. Then pupils and teacher discussed it without emotion and together decided how a repetition might be avoided.

The significant thing about the whole matter is that it was several weeks later that Miss X referred casually to the event. She had no intention of excusing the children's behavior nor of explaining her own part in the episode. She considered that the occasion had offered an opportunity to evaluate the appropriateness of their behavior. She thought that there was no reason to make them unhappy about their failure to manage their own affairs more effectually. To justify herself by blaming them or herself did not seemingly occur to her. In her mind the children's incapacity to prevent a break in their usual good control of themselves was not unlike their inability to read or to do a certain problem in arithmetic. She assumed no personal blame for that which they had not yet learned. Neither the teacher nor the pupils were made unhappy about the incident.

Miss X demonstrated her own emotional stability by never finding it necessary to resort to emotional outbursts. Often she was firm with the children, but she was never sarcastic, or harsh in her criticisms, or on the other hand effusive and demonstrative. She expressed no denouncing judgments upon people nor upon events, nor did she go into ecstasies over anything which transpired. Her demeanor was quiet and calm, but not apathetic.

Another evidence of her stability was the absence of strains and stresses in the classroom. Possessing a sense of humor, a clever little remark often changed a child's growing sullenness into a smile. Pupils were not encouraged to harbor resentment. Any dissatisfactions were immediately discussed and not permitted to lurk unnoticed by the teacher. All pupils were within the teacher's attention most of the time and her aim seemed to be that of preventing difficulties and misunderstandings. She sought no personal satisfactions, and if, in attempting to prevent conflict, she received a sullen answer or what might appear to be a saucy answer, she was unruffled.

Inclined to be constructive in her own outlook on life, she guided children's expression away from bias and unreasoning criticism. However, hers was no Pollyanna philosophy. Nor did she encourage this attitude in pupils. Rather, she tried to have them look for facts before expressing an emotionalized opinion. She herself displayed no narrow partisan views nor did she show any prejudices in her dealing with children of various nationalities. The obedient child was not always treated as if he were above reproof. The mischievous boy was accorded respect and consideration. In fact, each specific incident was judged on its merits, and there was no sweeping denunciation or all-engulfing praise.

This teacher never gave evidence of using the classroom as a place in which she was a superior individual because she was an adult. She expected courteous response from every child and usually got it. However, the feeling that actuated the response was of more interest to her than the language in which the response was cloaked. She did not demand, but she showed a questioning or surprised bearing if she were not treated with respect. As a result of her expectancy, pupils for the most part gave her the courtesy which she expected.

The following occasion suggests again Miss X's willingness and ability to meet children on their own level without demanding subservience because of her greater maturity.

Several boys who were late at noon reported that they had been looking for a lost ball. A discussion regarding an after-school penalty arose. One boy expressed an eagerness to get out to help his gang "beat up another kid and his gang." Miss X took twenty minutes to talk the difficulty through. She did not impose her point of view but tried to show the boys the wisdom of not getting stirred up needlessly.

They disagreed with her and held to their determination to fight it out. While respectful, they openly disagreed with her. A truce was suggested, and the teacher requested that they keep it until she could hear the other side of the argument. This they promised to do. The matter was closed temporarily with both boys and teacher willing to forget the matter and turn to the work of the afternoon.

Probably the reason for this teacher's unwillingness to impose her judgment upon youngsters and her independence of praise, recognition, or approval was that she had learned to think for herself. She trusted her own experience equally with that of others. She expressed an unwillingness to accept opinions of others until they had been tested. Many of her comments were those of an individual who has learned to think and act for herself. For instance, this teacher was wholly uninterested in a time schedule, as she thought it caused a feeling of futility because of the many unfinished tasks that were left suspended if working against time. She thought that this futility interfered with a teacher's ease and naturalness with her pupils. She was anxious to be as good a teacher as possible but wanted to judge for herself what contributed most to her own personal and professional growth. Her idea of self-improvement consisted in finding time to live, to enjoy the arts, to read, and to keep abreast of current events. She did not want any assumed responsibility to deprive her of time in her classroom during school hours. After school hours she wanted to study and enjoy social contacts. In other words, she knew what was good for her and wanted freedom to work through her own program.

Children who are to live and work in a democracy and be responsible for its functioning need to learn to think critically and to be discriminating. Pupils in Miss X's room were enjoying that privilege and practicing those very virtues because they had a teacher who considered their development in this direction her responsibility. She realized that it was her duty and privilege to keep herself free of prejudices which might be blinding. Her own determination to think and act for herself but with regard for others caused immature pupils to sense the fairness and wisdom of this course and to behave likewise. In their own words some of their reactions to the teacher and to their school experience are more convincing than further discussion of Miss X's influence upon her pupils.

"I like our room because the teacher always has good things planned, and the children do not cheat in the room or on the playground. Most of the children are nice to be with; they are fair and they are interesting to play with and talk with."

Miss X's second outstanding characteristic was stated as being her own personal resourcefulness. Her horizon was much broader than her own immediate environment. She read widely, took advantage of opportunities to increase her understanding of world events, and tried to acquaint herself with the facts of political and governmental activity. She listened to the radio broadcasts of news and of comments on the news. She was concerned with the literary events and musical happenings within the community and was a regular participant in community affairs. In other words, she was an active, well-informed, and interested citizen.

This interest was carried into the classroom. Children were invited to tell about the radio programs which they enjoyed. Whenever broadcasts of an educational nature were scheduled for school hours, pupils and teacher listened and later discussed their reactions. It was not at all unusual to have children suggest at the close of the school day that there would be a particularly good program broadcast during the evening which all should hear. These broadcasts were mentioned with as much enthusiasm as were playground activities. In fact, when the pupils were asked what appealed to them most about their school and their class, many spoke of the broadcasts they heard and were helped by the teacher to understand.

Miss X appreciated uniqueness and differences in children. She tried to encourage them to express their own thoughts and emotions freely and without restraint. Being talented musically herself, she helped children to compose simple melodies and write words which carried the mood of the music. Naturally all children did not have the ability to do original compositions with music and with words. Often one child could create a simple melody but could not express the theme of the melody in words. Another child would be urged to try his hand at the words. In this way group or class attempts at developing their own operettas or plays were incited.

Miss X had experienced the joy of expressing herself in one or more of the arts and knew when and how to encourage pupils. By skillful suggestion she seemed able to give a pupil whose courage was waning a necessary lift over the hard spot. Not given to superfluous praise and commendation, pupils appreciated Miss X's approval and encouragement. They knew that the praise was sincere and genuine and knew further that it was deserved. It seemed to make them alert to the contributions of their fellow pupils. It was not at all infrequent to hear remarks such as these:

"Miss X, see what George has done. Isn't it good?"

"This is the best drawing Helen has ever made."

"Mary's song is beautiful. I would like to write one as good as hers."

The atmosphere of this particular classroom seemed to be confidence-inspiring. Applause and approval were not given gratuitously but were generously bestowed when earned. Children wanted to earn it and frequently did, but it often was bestowed privately or by mere nod or facial expression. When a pupil was laboring over a drawing or a story, his spirit was visibly restored by an understanding smile from the teacher. This insight which Miss X possessed because of her own experience was a real support to children who were exploring the untried. The spiritual kindredness which strengthened the understanding between teacher and pupil was apparent.

Not only were the exceptional talents of pupils fostered in this classroom, but the feelings of children were appraised with as much insight and accorded as much concern as their endowments. The cultural assets of this teacher were not only those which come with constructive use of leisure and development of abilities, but they had enriched her appreciation of people and their human needs. Miss X had learned that children need to feel secure if they are to expose their thoughts and particularly their feelings. Her own living had made her sensitive to these needs of others as well as capable of shaping an environment to meet these needs.

A typical illustration of her regard for a child's feelings and for the need for preserving her self-respect is the following:

A child had brought a book from home to ask whether it was a good book to read in school. Miss X said that she was not familiar with the book but would look it over. Upon glancing at it she discovered that it was a very cheap edition of a completely undesirable series. She did not allow the child to sense any criticism but asked her if she thought it wise to spend time in reading about one group of characters for a whole series when there were so many good things to read. "I'll tell you: let's work it out together. You read a chapter, and we will talk it over to see whether we like it." The child was perfectly satisfied to read the one chapter and then take the book back home again without feeling humiliated because of her poor choice.

That a rich experiential background contributes directly to a teacher's desire to have pupils know reality in a vivid and unprejudiced way is substantiated by Miss X's own statement about her life as a growing child and as a teacher:

"As a child I had the opportunity of being in a home in which there were older brothers and sisters. Our home was a center for friends of both my brothers and sisters and my parents. We lived in a small community and as a family shared not only in community life but in the joys and sorrows of our neighbors. I learned as a growing child to know people and to feel a sense of responsibility for understanding them and for participating in their lives. I think all children should learn to understand others and to be sympathetically inclined toward what others do.

"I can recall occasions when I visited in homes in which there were suffering and strain. These experiences made it clear to me that individuals need to acquire for themselves the power to withstand shocks and vital changes in life without being cut down mentally and spiritually. Young people should learn to face the facts of life directly. I have been grateful as an adult that I saw realities of life as a child. As a teacher I bring as much of life into my class as I can.

"Children themselves have had a definite influence upon my standards. Those coming from homes economically independent as well as those from poorer homes have all needed to have their ideals reconciled, home teachings and self-discoveries made outside of the home interpreted, and group problems analyzed and made clear. What one teaches depends upon what children's problems introduce. Every class group is different and the members have to learn to work together as a social group. This means building a set of standards for conduct which all members of the group can understand and reach. Children's reactions, their ideas and opinions, have taught me to work through from several outlooks to common goals for all. An understanding of how to work in a social group is essential to all successful accomplishment."

The expansiveness of the personality of a teacher has an immediate effect upon pupils. Miss X's classroom manner was cordial and friendly. Any visitor to the classroom was received as a guest in a home. Unlike the restraint a visitor feels in the teacher upon entry into the classroom, a cheery welcome was immediately forthcoming from Miss X. The visitor was presented to the pupils, his identity made known, and he was invited to share in whatever was in progress. The pupils were not treated as unhearing, unseeing, and uninterested bystanders, but were brought into the conversation and accepted as co-hosts and co-hostesses. The naturalness of the whole situation relieved any probable tension and made it possible for the work of the classroom to proceed without disturbance and without confusion on the part of children, teacher, or visitor. The teacher's social poise and security are reflected in pupils who approach a newly introduced visitor with ease and unembarrassment to ask him whether he would be interested in something going on in another corner of the classroom. This gesture of friendliness and courtesy was the rule rather than the exception in Miss X's class.

The abandonment of self-consciousness on the part of her pupils was undoubtedly due to the conversational manner which Miss X used with her children. Possessing an ever-ready sense of humor, she chanced such remarks as these with no fear of losing her dignity or of receiving discourteous responses:

"John, won't you give me a chance to talk when you know how much I like to talk?" or "Give me the recipe for a good teacher. I want to know so that I can be one." Or again, "Your foot rhythm is good but your mouth rhythm is poor. How do you account for it?"

The children laughingly responded to direct correction when cloaked in language which they enjoyed. Instead of provoking ill-temper or impudence, her humor caused smiles and a willingness to take suggestions. There seemed to be friendly response to the teacher's good humor and unwillingness to be disturbed by minor infractions. There was little bickering or quarreling among the pupils, but a readiness to enjoy jokes on each other and graciously to accept a joke upon themselves.

Miss X had an unlimited supply of incidents upon which she could call to elicit pupils' interest. Her extensive reading and social proclivities made her a good conversationalist. She frequently entertained her pupils with interesting episodes from literature and stories about well-known people. She made them acquainted with famous personalities and enriched their background for reading. Being familiar with the stories which they read and told, she could prompt their memories and add incidents which they had forgotten or overlooked. As a consequence of her familiarity with their stories, the children took delight in talking with Miss X about what they were reading. Like her, they showed an unusual interest in books and in dramatical portrayal of their stories. Several different pupils in the classroom, when asked what they liked best about school, said that it was the most interesting term they had ever had, because the teacher knew so many people and amusing stories. "It's fun going to school," said one, "because there is so much to do and so much to learn. Our teacher lets us do so many different things. We listen to the radio, make up plays, write stories, do arithmetic, and best of all have so many good books to read and talk about. I like it all very much."

The expansiveness of Miss X with her own personal resources made her a stimulating personality for children to be associated with. They, as she, became appreciative of the life about them and found channels for satisfying expression in music, drama, literature, and in learning to know and understand people better.

The third characterizing quality of this teacher was her interest in people in general, but particularly in children. Her interest in them was not as subjects to be taught, but as individualities and potential personalities to be developed. Her ability to establish and maintain rapport with children was such as is rarely found. This was probably due to her complete freedom from dependence upon their reactions to her personally. She seemed to have no inclination to satisfy her own emotions through them. She was frank to say that, while she did want children to like her, she was more concerned with studying them as reacting individuals than in securing any particular kind of response from them. To a question regarding her obvious understanding of children's responses, Miss X said that she enjoyed studying her pupils and tried to anticipate what the effect of her own expression would be upon them. This thoughtfulness was observable in Miss X's deliberateness and poise. She never let herself be hurried or harassed by pressing detail but maintained always a quiet, calm, but cheery manner in the classroom. She never let herself get to the place where she was obliged to relieve any pent-up emotion at the expense of the children. Her classroom was never the scene of tension due to her own inability to see herself objectively. She studied herself and the children with deliberation before acting.

The pupils in the room were likewise relatively free from strain. The teacher's alertness to developing tenseness and her ready humor prevented any rising ill feeling. If one child showed a tendency to be critical of another, she was quick to turn his attention to himself through some remembered incident about him. Instead of the critic's placing the child he was about to criticize in an unfavorable light, his attention was diverted. Invariably the criticizing pupil had time to "quiet down" and forget his criticism. This steering the child away from conflict was practiced only when the issues were personal and when the children were aroused emotionally. Sincere differences of opinion were encouraged and discussed as long as was necessary for an understanding to be reached. Miss X's own opinion was that sane and clear thinking were impossible when an individual was under stress of emotional disturbance.

There were no sarcastic nor insinuating remarks used in this teacher's classroom. The visitor saw evidences of a respect for pupils' personalities in the teacher's manner of dealing with pupils and in the regard with which pupils held each other. The teacher might adjust her comments to fit an occasion, but, if regard for the feelings of each other is not built up through a regular and consistent effort on the part of the teacher, pupils will not have it imbued in them. Miss X's pupils knew of each other's weaknesses and talked about them but with a kindliness which bespoke the absence of superiority or condescension. There was no evidence of any spirit of self-righteousness.

The pupils in this room talked freely with the teacher about their interests and their hobbies. She knew their play habits, their hours of rest, their friends outside of school. For the most part, she was acquainted with their mothers and let the children know that the school and home were united in their interest. Always the parents and home were accorded utmost respect in spite of known deficiencies. With a natural enthusiasm some particularly encouraging feature of his home environment was held before each child, eliminating, as much as possible, any self-consciousness he might feel about his home's shortcomings as contrasted with the home situations of other pupils. The constructive influence of this one bit of teacher insight was indicated by the naturalness and unrestraint with which the pupils shared so many of their joys and sorrows with the teacher.

The child who had a poor home environment or one who had not yet learned to adjust without seeking attention was particularly challenging to Miss X. She considered it her responsibility so to shape the school environment that each child had the kind stimulation and guidance which he needed most. She had a way of enlisting the help of other pupils in bringing to bear the influences needed by the several members of the class. For example, she planned with the chairman of one group to have a shy, sensitive member of the group take a place of leadership. With another chairman she arranged for a boy who could not draw to be teamed with one who liked to draw and yet was sufficiently patient with the former's inability to encourage him to try. To the child who showed a tendency to be antisocial, she gave the responsibility of planning a party with a group of boys and girls. In other words, behavior reactions were as much planned and steered as were reading or arithmetic study, and yet in such an unobjectionable way as not to be apparent. Resistance was avoided by planning rather than by omission of constructive treatment.

Intelligent children respond to recognized self-accomplishment. Pupils in Miss X's room said that they liked their classroom because they "learned lots." They felt good about their own learning in addition to responding pleasantly to Miss X as a person. Antagonisms were so conspicuously absent that there was little in their school experience that produced any unpleasantness. Accomplishment was associated with pleasant surroundings and therefore was satisfying to a marked degree. And this satisfaction was remembered by children who had been taught by Miss X long after they had left her classroom. Several boys and girls, two years after leaving the school in which she taught, were asked to name their favorite teacher. All but one out of a group of sixteen named Miss X, saying that they liked being in her room better than in any other because they thought that they learned more and because in

Miss X's room the pupils seemed to like each other better.

Miss X thus affected the thinking and social outlook of the pupils who came in contact with her. She was personally able to maintain a classroom environment which exerted a positive and pleasant influence upon not only self-learning but also upon social learning. The persons who were part of the learning situation were appreciated and liked by each other. Democracy was at work in her classroom. Without defining the exact tasks performed, it is fair to say that group purposes were furthered because of the pleasant and satisfying interactions of the persons composing the group.

CHAPTER VI

FOR TEACHERS IN SERVICE

Out of this study of teacher-pupil relationships grow some pertinent suggestions for teachers in service. There are some ways in which teachers can examine their personal effectiveness and through so doing seek to improve their teaching. There is also the possibility of teachers' becoming just self-analytical and thereby defeating the very purpose of their effort. Enough has been said up to this point to establish the fact that an individual's teaching behavior is determined by that which he feels and thinks, that which actuates his speech and all other outward expressions of inner convictions. In other words, the teacher's classroom behavior represents the sum total of all that he has experienced and is experiencing personally. The error which might be made is to conceive of teacher behavior as something that can be improved immediately. Its roots go far too deep for that to happen. If the teacher sets about to make his own classroom manner conform to any pattern, no matter how good the pattern, teacher-pupil relationships are not likely to be substantially improved, for outer manifestations are but reflections or concomitants and not directly improvable to any great extent.

The question then arises—What is a reasonable course for the teacher to pursue to increase his effectiveness? To this question there are many possible answers which might be offered. A relatively long and somewhat intensive study of the reasons for the effectiveness of teachers prompts the proposal of the following as requirements of successful teaching.

1. Because the teacher is working with human beings, he needs to understand the psychology of growth in general and in particular that stage of growth of the pupils with whom he is associated. He needs to know how learning takes place and how to translate his own knowledge into the interests of the learners that their interests may be used to further desirable learning.

2. Although teaching is an art, it is also a skill which requires a ready, working knowledge of the materials of the profession, particularly of that area of teaching in which one is engaged. This entails familiarity with the literature as well as practical proficiency. It means that today the teacher should have a liberal education as a foundation with pertinent and continuous professional education while in service.

3. The kind of education that has been herein taken for granted requires, particularly at the elementary level, interest and appreciation; first, in all of the arts, and second, proficiency in teaching and basic techniques in one or more of the art fields. Of all teachers are demanded an alertness to the things of the spirit

and an appreciation of artistic expression when or where it is found. The teacher should possess at least the artistic spirit and be aesthetically sensitive.

4. The teacher needs to be socially competent, having learned to take his place in adult groups. He should know how to adjust to other adults without surrendering his own convictions. His work throws him into daily contact with persons not of his own selection. Part of his success as a member of a teaching group depends upon his ability to associate himself with other teachers in advancing his profession through improving its practices.

5. Since the teacher is, as has been developed in previous chapters, a personal exemplification of the culture he would advance, in addition to being an active agent in the culture afforded by the classroom, he needs to know thoroughly the problems as well as the ideals of the society in which he lives. This means that the present-day American teacher, irrespective of the age level of the pupils he teaches, should know how American democracy is functioning or failing to function through participation in it and through a continuing interest and appraisal of the vital social issues of the day.

Before developing each of these five proposals somewhat in detail, it should be made clear that these factors are suggested for direct improvement rather than for the teacher's classroom behavior. If the teacher will interpret the implications of these five factors for him-

self and then proceed to increase his assets, he is likely
to find wherein he can strengthen his own teaching
equipment. Through the process of evaluating his own
qualifications and then with enthusiasm and determination setting about to broaden his experience, he
will acquire an increasing personal positiveness, based
on understanding, which should contribute to his effectiveness as a person and as a teacher. This kind of
self-improvement is the only kind advocated, for it
alone can result in increased personal direction and
control which augment an individual's motive force. It
requires effort and consistency, but it will be the
directed purposing itself which will make the teacher
a more dynamic classroom teacher.

1. PSYCHOLOGY OF GROWTH

Much more is known about the facts of growth now
than was known a few years ago. There have been
made available for teachers the results of the research
in child psychology which has been in progress in
several well-established clinical centers both in this
country and abroad. Out of the systematic studies and
observation of children of varying age levels certain
significant findings regarding growth and development
are now accepted. It is highly important that those
responsible for the education of children, both parents
and teachers, have some familiarity with these principles. Intelligent guidance will be facilitated if adults
who are associating with growing children possess

enough fundamental information about their growth tendencies to know what to expect and how to provide situations which will promote optimum learning.

Extended discussion of the psychology of growth is here impossible. References will be included at the close of the chapter which will afford the reader opportunity for getting a more complete overview of the whole field of child study. The purpose here is to bring to the attention of the teacher a few of the more basic principles of growth with which he should be familiar. While experienced teachers are probably more or less aware of exhibited characteristics of children of different maturity levels, they may not have realized the serial order of growth and the need for protecting the natural interaction of the child and his environment.

Growth is continuous and unbroken but more rapid at some periods of the child's life than at others. The body growth rate is extremely rapid from birth to approximately two years of age. From that point on the rate slowly decreases to about the age of ten, when there is another rapid pickup from about ten to sixteen years of age. Children enter school in approximately the middle of the two to ten-year age period, at a time when some of the results of rapid growth are being consolidated. While the strains which accompany rapid growth have somewhat subsided, the child's world is being so definitely broadened as far as social contacts are concerned that the teacher needs to be particularly careful to watch all phases or aspects of development. Strains of social adjustment may affect emotional development, and both may have a direct bearing upon the physical. During this period the child's rate of metabolism is high with a consequent tendency to excitability. It is very necessary, if this emotional stability is to be guarded, that the child not be permitted to overdo physically. Alternating periods of rest and activity are desirable and need to be regularly arranged.

At the several times during the child's school life when his bodily-growth rate changes from that of comparative slowness to increased rapidity, his psychological stability may be subject to great strain. This is particularly true at adolescence when the physical aspects of growth outstrip those of social and emotional maturation. The complexities of such a condition, both for the child himself and for the teacher, are too specific to be dealt with generally. Mention is made of this condition simply to call attention to the point that a teacher cannot deal sympathetically and understandingly with a child if he is not aware of the changing physical, emotional, and social needs of that child. The successful teacher will know the interrelatedness of the several aspects of growth as well as the sequence or serial order of growth.

Environmental factors too play a large part in the development of all human beings. While the school can do little about the factors of heredity and nutrition, it can make a real contribution to the influence of environment in the total education of children. It may be unable to change poor home environment, but it can supplement the home environment in such a way that all children may have some of the more wholesome influences which those of more privileged environments enjoy, particularly the aesthetic qualities which stimulate sensitiveness to beauty in all its forms. Again, however, the teacher's insight and resourcefulness will determine how wisely the supplementation will be made. If, in addition to being sensitive to the arts, the teacher is a student of the sciences and of social conditions and problems, he will be much better able to analyze the environment in which the nurture of the growing child is taking place. He will have to be realistic in his outlook upon life and keep abreast with the ever-changing conditions which the means of rapid communication, the radio, the movies,, and the many forms of transportation are bringing about. He will have to be the kind of student who studies but who also tests his reading by personal observation and by keeping himself open-minded and flexible. The teacher who shuts his eyes to the things of the environment is no match for even the six-year-old in a world of rapid change. Studies quoted at the end of the chapter suggest the importance of environment in the nurture and development of wholesome growth.

Every child who has a provocative environment has some interests which are peculiarly his own. Younger children in school are usually given opportunities to express these interests, particularly in the early primary years. Very soon, however, in some schools the press of work to be accomplished causes teachers to overlook children's interests. All too often what the child is expected to do in school is imposed, not because the teacher intends to dominate but because the teacher feels obligated to see that the children get a certain amount of work done. Without deliberately trying to supplant the pupils' interests which have been aroused by play or reading, either within school or outside of school, the teacher sometimes overlooks chances of using children's play interests as a basis for extension of school interest. Since children of given age and experience levels have been found to have certain rather characteristic interest trends, irrespective of locality, it is helpful to know what these are. If, then, instead of overlooking these natural tendencies and thus unintentionally thwarting them, the teacher builds upon them, he is utilizing that which is a stimulus to action.

During the first two or three years in school, children like to indulge in dramatic play. They like to pretend and to imitate. Toys, animals, and simple objects of endless variety enter into their dramatic play. Making simple puppets with which they enact the scenes of adult activities consume hours of the time of some of the children of this age. Others dress themselves up and go through the motions of keeping house, playing store or school, or imitating the work of the milkman, policeman, and other adult contributors in the society of which they are a part. Active and vigorous spontaneous games occupy children of this age.

As they mature, children grow into the collecting stage and take pride in personal collections. Their games become less imitative and increasingly competitive in character. Personal skill and group rivalry are manifest in the boy's place in a group or gang, and in the girl's social recognition in a group of her own choice. The preadolescent's satisfaction is greatest when he can prove his place with his peers. His outlook is beyond himself, and so his pleasures are more social than egocentric. His sense of pride in accomplishment, if the accomplishment gives him status with those of his own sex, leads him to a display of prowess in some particular kind of physical, social, or mental endeavor.

Gradually personal adornment interests girls while boys of the same age may still be interested in sports and their own physical strength. However, as the youth reaches adolescence, he wants to be successful, to show off a bit possibly, or in some way attract the attention of the opposite sex. He is fearful of ridicule and so acts often in ways which are strange even to himself. He is interested at this period in what makes people successful, often attaching himself in fantasy to some person or ideal to which he wishes to give his loyalty. Life intrigues him, and he is interested in it for the first time as a person. Novels, motion pictures, drama, and other roles of escape allow the adolescent to project himself into life as it is imagined.

Only the adult who can understand and not scoff or belittle is permitted a place in these sacred precincts of childhood and youth. The discerning teacher will watch for these proclivities, a very few of which have been suggested above, as hints for patterning school pursuits. Much of the subject matter of the school curriculum can be approached with success and with interest on the part of pupils in these several periods of maturity if the motivating social and emotional drives of the period are used as leverages.

2. THE TEACHER'S PROFESSIONAL EQUIPMENT

Education for living in the world of the twentieth century demands all of the scholarship of previous centuries. Teachers need more than ever before to have as liberal an education as they can get. They need grounding in the humanities and as wide knowledge as they are capable of acquiring in the sciences, both natural and physical as well as social. The complexity and impersonality of the present-day cultural pattern require keen critical ability to discriminate between the enduring and fleeting values. Only the perspective gained by a knowledge of history can help the teacher to know relationships in their true light. Today's teacher cannot have too much general education unless in the process of getting that education he loses sight of the plight of the uneducated and deprived individual or has his human sympathies dulled by living too long in a realm shielded from the reality of the contemporaneous social scene. The teacher's general education should never be considered as finished. He must strive continually to get all information available that will help him to comprehend more intelligently the cause-and-effect relations in modern life.

But as has been said before in this chapter, the teacher has a peculiar challenge to meet in translating his own knowledge into the curriculum needs of pupils of a given age. There are techniques and ways of doing this that have proved their effectiveness. The teacher's professional skill will depend upon the extent to which he can incorporate his own knowledge and experience into ways of expression which will intrigue his pupils into wanting to know. His skill in setting the stage for learning, in selecting appropriate materials of instruction, in guiding his pupils' thinking through the use of these materials, and then in helping them to evaluate their own efforts will determine his skill as an instructor. To aid the prospective teacher in matters of instruction, professional schools expose him to the evolutionary history of educational theory and method. The teacher's personal responsibility is to bring to focus in his own procedures information, method, and knowledge of the learner in such a way that he practices the best-known theories of education.

Since, as has been stated again and again in this book, the teacher must personify that which he teaches, it is reasonable to add that he can apply only such method as he can incorporate into his own actions. He may have studied about the very latest discovered method for effectively teaching children to spell, but, if he has to refer to the "recipe book," the prepared statement regarding this method, his pupils will not wait for him to combine the ingredients. He can teach only that which he can demonstrate. His own thinking must be clear before he can teach others to think clearly. In other words, professional education produces results when it affects the thinking, feeling, and acting of the teacher and then only. If it fails to do this, it is professional information untranslated by the teacher into teaching skill.

Just as equipment and materials used in other practical pursuits become outmoded, so in education old and antiquated books, maps, and other teaching equipment need to be superseded by newer and more up-to-date materials of instruction. The use of radio, slides, the motion picture, and the various sound-transmitting instruments have opened up new ways of teaching which the teacher cannot afford to disregard. It is the teacher's obligation to keep himself informed and acquainted with modern equipment and modern methods of instruction. While commercial companies, for purposes of business, carry to the teacher the new visual and auditory devices, the teacher should take the initiative in checking upon the results of the use of these aids. Every teacher who would be well informed and would give his pupils the benefit of educational research should know where and how to find the reported investigations of other educators. There is a rich field of educational literature which is open to any teacher who will take the time to use it. The place of newer materials as well as improvements in method are well covered in articles and books listed for teachers in the *Education Index,* a current record of contributions to the field of education. Professional education is thus continuous for the teacher who would grow in his knowledge of better ways of teaching.

If the teacher understands the psychology of growth, has a good general educational background, and keeps abreast of the best educational thought, he should be able to recognize a psychologically sound curriculum and be instrumental in setting into motion such a curriculum. He should feel secure in trusting his own judgment as to what constitutes desirable learning for children of given experiential backgrounds and known potential abilities. He should be able to apply such tests and measures of learning as to give him a complete evaluation of the effectiveness of the curriculum. He should know whether sound mental attitudes and good bodily development as well as desirable social relationships are accompanying the mastery of the common integrating skills and knowledges. He should know how well pupils can attack and think through

problems and how much individual talents and apti-
tudes are being fostered by his program of instruction.

Unless the teacher's independence in studying professional problems has reached the place where he can
investigate for himself and feel reasonably confident of
his own discriminating judgment, he is not ready to
fulfill the demands of the modern school. The time
is past in education when prescription and regimenta-
tion dictate. The curriculum has expanded to include
life in its many complexities. Creative, independent
thought based upon critical thinking and experience
are the expected outcomes of the expanding curriculum. The teacher is considered in the emerging school
to be an educational statesman. More and more important decisions are left to the teacher. An adequate
professional equipment is absolutely necessary for the
teacher who would assume in full measure the privileges being extended to him.

3. THE AESTHETIC SPIRIT

All children are sensitive to their surroundings. Individual children, however, differ greatly in their
sensory acuity. Too often the child's native sensitiveness is permitted to be the barometer for the educational effort that is directed in his behalf. If upon
school entrance he shows a readiness to give expression
to his impressions, he is encouraged to do so. The child
who shows little or no tendency toward expression is
sometimes allowed to drift along with no attempt be-

ing made to increase his impressionability. While it must be recognized that there are limits beyond which education cannot go, it is extremely doubtful if the school has really made aesthetic development one of its major aims. It has failed to seriously consider what might be done to make children more sensitive to beauty in its many forms. The great variation in native capacity complicates the teaching problem but does not make it impossible.

If teachers themselves were all sensitive to the beauties with which they are surrounded, the first step would be taken in the nurturing of a generation of American children who were somewhat discriminating in their taste. If teachers all enjoyed listening to good music, hearing good plays, seeing good paintings, and reading good literature, it is not unlikely that their pupils might know that there were such things to be enjoyed. If teachers performed musically, danced, took part in dramas, wrote verse and prose, painted, drew, or composed music, again their pupils might be fired by their teachers' enthusiasms to do likewise. If either or both of these alternatives were realities, there probably would be less question about whether children were being helped to become sensitive to the creative efforts of others and, in all probability, appreciative of the results of these efforts.

But teachers, like children, have not been exposed enough to the beauties of sound, color, and arrangement and have not been given the necessary guidance to become discriminating. The eye and the ear have to be trained to exclude as well as to include if true appreciation is to result. The very word "appreciation" infers a choice. It is practice in making choices that has been omitted in the education of many adults, in which group fall many teachers.

The school curriculum today includes art, music, and bodily rhythm, but it is only the discriminating teacher who can help pupils see, let alone faithfully record, their impressions or an interpretation of their impressions. Many more teachers who have had guidance in art appreciation, who are sensitive to harmonious sound, and who have the acquired grace of body or who know how to assist others to gain it are needed in the schools. Teachers should be concert goers, frequent attendants at art exhibits, and interested and acquainted with the dance. Their enthusiasm for these pleasures might then be transmitted to the children in their classes.

Often children's expression is hampered by teachers who cannot help them and encourage them in their creative efforts. Every teacher would profit by being a member of a studio workshop of some description. Talent in all forms of expression is rare and not expected of teachers. Talent with one medium of expression is desirable. Experience in trying to express self is practically a necessity and should be expected of all teachers who are responsible for the basic education of children.

Literature is an open road to the better understanding and appreciation of human emotions. The innermost feelings of which most persons are at some time capable are revealed on the pages of literature. Autobiography is a self-revelation of human motives, aspirations, and defeats. Biography and fiction are disclosures of assumed emotions. The reading of all three of these literary forms broadens the sympathies of readers. Teachers especially can make themselves more understanding of the problems of youth by wide reading as well as extending the horizons of their own interests and experiences. If teachers are to inculcate a love of good reading, they should know the benefits to be derived therefrom.

For pure enjoyment and the lightening of the spirit, the pleasures of the theater, the concert, and the recital are worth the teacher's effort. They have a positive effect on the emotional tone and make the teacher a happier person for children's company.

The aesthetic spirit is delicate. It cannot be hurt and expected to survive. It does not thrive with requirement or obligation. It needs freedom and encouragement. Only one who is nicely sensitive himself can support and help to sustain that sensitiveness in others.

Making all children write poetry or pretend to be enthralled by some musical rendition is not the proper way to foster creativity or sensitivity. They require a far gentler treatment, treatment that is born of a spiritual understanding which accompanies common experience.

4. SOCIAL COMPETENCY

Most teachers are well beyond the average in social competency. They are among the group of people who have diversified interests and who make an effort to broaden their outlook through social participation. They realize that they need to know the viewpoints of others and so seek to contact those in other walks of life. Teachers participate in civic undertakings and do their part to further community enterprise. Teachers are often sought as leaders of civic groups, and from time immemorial they have been associated with that which is cultural in the community.

Teachers can know more intimately the home and community environments of their pupils if they participate actively in affairs of the community and mingle freely with the adults of the community. Without first-hand contact with the parents of their pupils it is difficult for teachers to supplement individual children's experiences. Parent-teacher associations offer one opportunity for teachers to become acquainted with parents, but all pupils' parents are not members of P. T. A. groups. The parents who do not avail themselves of this way of knowing their children's teachers need to be contacted through other channels. Occasional home visits by the teacher will be helpful and will afford a better understanding of the school by the home. Since visitation will take the teacher into all types of homes, it will improve relations materially if the teacher is capable of meeting each parent in a direct person-to-person manner. This requires unusual social facility on the part of the teacher as he will be obliged to adapt himself to people of varying social experience and sensitivity.

Participation in civic enterprise or in professional organizations may subject the teacher to discussion of controversial issues. As a citizen and as an adult outside of the classroom, the teacher is entitled to free expression of his own opinions and convictions. However, if he is vigorous in declaring his own convictions, he will have to assure others of his professional integrity in not imposing his personal views on immature minds. It is a direct challenge to the intelligence and good judgment of the teacner to be able to take his place in adult groups and at the same time keep himself above reproach as an open-minded, fair, and impartial teacher. Social competency of a high order is demanded by these requirements. The teacher must always keep the respect of both parents and children if his effectiveness is to be preserved.

5. Understanding American Democracy

If teachers are going to teach children to understand the problems and processes of American democracy, they themselves will need to be able to call upon a knowledge of economics, government, and sociology, as well as geography and history. Interpretation of modern problems of production, exchange, distribution, consumption, and conservation cannot be attempted by the teacher who does not have a background of information. Problems of labor, unemployment, crime, poverty, delinquency, and possible social security are part and parcel of the cultural pattern which has to be wrestled with first by teachers before they can help their pupils to take a beginning step in gaining a comprehensive picture of the present. Although pupils will not be expected to discuss with intelligence the intricacies of these perplexing issues until they reach the college level, the elementary social-studies curriculum is concerned with affording children fundamental experience for coping with governmental and sociological issues. Every teacher is a guide in this social experiencing. The teacher should know American culture both past and present. The story of the evolution of American institutions is one with which maturing American children should not only be familiar but in which they should take justifiable pride. Children should also be acquiring a real knowledge of the physical and natural setting in which these American institutions have developed. They should know something of the history of community life in America and be aware of the interrelations of industry. They should realize the interdependence of the United States with the rest of the world. The teacher will have to guide them into meaningful study of these several phases of national development while helping them to comprehend the disturbed international order of friendliness among nations.

Transportation and communication changes interest and intrigue children. It is not enough for them to know that there have been changes. They should grasp the reasons for such change and the contribution of science to changed social procedures. They should be helped to understand that change can be expected and that technological advances will cause man to alter even his present ways of living. They should see the necessity for employing science in improving conditions of health, sanitation, and housing. Teachers will have to make children realize that in America everyone should have an opportunity to share in the necessities of life and to have some measure of security.

The relation of wise conservation of forests, water, power, and mineral resources to the general welfare of American citizens is a concept that teachers need to acquire themselves and to help their pupils grasp. The problems that are involved in this social issue are far from being solved now. Generations to come may have to develop legislation which will insure a more equitable distribution of America's rich natural resources. Today's children will be concerned as adults with the difficulties involved in social legislation which attempts to control this great perplexing problem.

Democratic institutions will not be perpetuated without constant vigilance on the part of an alert citizenry. Such institutions will not continue of their own momentum. Freedom of speech, freedom of the press, and the personal right of the individual to live his life free from domination and restraint, providing he does his part to preserve the common weal have been won and preserved by effort. Humanitarian culture is under constant fire today, and the freedoms of the American people are threatened. Children should be made to see the relationship between democracy in the classroom and democracy at large. The teacher's task in democracy's behalf is real. The teacher beyond all others has a laboratory for the practice of democratic living. He can illustrate for immature minds the kind of personal give-and-take that is necessary for a functioning democracy. The children's world with which the teacher is entrusted is sufficiently circumscribed for the processes of democracy to be made real and tangible. It is no wonder that it is said that the defense of American democracy is in its schools.

Thoughtful American citizens need to know how to find and to use information and to distinguish between what are facts and what are distorted facts or propaganda. The school has the responsibility for teaching children to find and to use information, to observe critically, and to evaluate activities of a social nature in terms of their ultimate effect upon personal freedom and individual well-being. If teachers can cause pupils to form the habit of suspending their decisions until all possible evidence has been weighed and then of acting in the light of their best judgment, reasoning citizens will be in the making. This will be a genuine contribution to the future of American democracy. For teachers this means the giving of guidance in simple research and training in the habits of orderly and systematic thinking.

Teachers will need to be convinced of the morality of the democratic life. They will have to feel keenly that it is worth the best that one can offer. Without conviction, certainty, and steadfastness an enthusiasm for democratic living will not be transmitted from teacher to pupil. The cause of democratic institutions cannot be championed effectively by lukewarm regard. There can be but one way of life presented to American children as the right way of life if they are to be the future upholders of the faith in American principles.

Statements made above may seem extreme. The needs are stated emphatically, but there is no intention of under-estimating the zeal for improvement which actuates most teachers. As a whole, teachers are professionally minded and, if anything, overconscientious in their desire to become better teachers. This is the very reason for setting a course to be run which has no goal to be reached and to be clung to with finality. It is the process and spirit of growth which are important. Even the adjudged effective teacher can make himself more effective. If the teacher attempts to look at himself to evaluate his worth as a teacher, he is centering his attention on a cause rather than a result. His success has to be measured by looking at his pupils. If they are learning to live more effectively, he may then think that possibly he is an effective teacher.

The foregoing five areas of growth are suggested because they offer broad fields for effort. If some of the activities are undertaken with consistency and with enthusiasm, teachers should be happier persons themselves and more stimulating adults for children's learning environment.

SELECTED READINGS

BURNHAM, W. H.—*Great Teachers and Mental Health*. New York: D. Appleton and Company, 1926.

BURNHAM, W. H.—*The Normal Mind*. New York: D. Appleton and Company, 1926.

BURNHAM, W. H.—*The Wholesome Personality*. New York: D. Appleton and Company, 1931.

Child Development and the Curriculum. Thirty-eighth Year Book, Part I, N. S. S. E. Bloomington, Illinois: Public School Publishing Company, 1939.

COUNTS, GEORGE S.—*The Social Foundations of Education*. New York: Charles Scribner's Sons, 1934.

Creative Expression. Progressive Education Association (Gertrude Hartman and Ann Shumaker, Editors). New York: The John Day Company, 1932.

CURTI, M. W.—*Child Psychology*. New York: Longmans, Green and Company, 1931.

DEWEY, JOHN—*Experience and Education*. New York: The Macmillan Company, 1938.

FOLLETT, M. P.—*Creative Experience*. New York: Longmans, Green and Company, 1924.

HOCKETT, JOHN A., and JACOBSEN, E. W.—*Modern Practices in the Elementary School*. New York: Ginn and Company, 1938.

LANE, ROBERT H.—*The Teacher in the Modern Elementary School*. Boston: Houghton Mifflin Company, 1941.

LEE, J. MURRAY, and LEE, MAY.—*The Child and His Curriculum*. New York: D. Appleton-Century Company, 1940.

MARSHALL, LEON C., and GOETZ, RACHEL M.—*Curriculum Making in the Social Studies*. Part XIII. Report of the Commission on Social Studies, American Historical Society. New York: Charles Scribner's Sons, 1936.

MUMFORD, LEWIS—*Faith for Living*. New York: The Macmillan Company, 1940.

Newer Instructional Practices of Promise. The Department of Supervisors and Directors of Instruction of the National Education Association, 1939.

PRESCOTT, DANIEL—*Emotion and the Educative Process*. American Council on Education, 1938.

STUDEBAKER, J. W.—*The American Way*. New York: McGraw-Hill Book Company, 1935.

The Teacher and Society. Yearbook I, John Dewey Society. New York: D. Appleton-Century, 1937.

Utilization of Community Resources in the Social Studies. Cambridge, Mass.: National Council for the Social Studies, Ninth Yearbook, 1938.

Teachers Digest. 407 Grand Avenue, Des Moines, Iowa. (Monthly Review of Professional Literature)

CHAPTER VII

EVALUATING THE TEACHER'S PERSONAL EFFECTIVENESS

The foregoing chapters have been devoted to descriptions of effective and noneffective teachers. The reasons for their contrasting success in stimulating and guiding children's all-round development have been suggested. The caution should be made again, however, that there is no definite pattern for the effective teacher. According to the interpreted findings of this relatively extended study of teacher-pupil relationships, the teacher's effectiveness can be determined best by noting and analyzing pupils' responses to the teacher's conduct. Recurring responses on the part of pupils to observed likeness in behavior on the part of teachers have inspired a rating scale for attempting the evaluation of a teacher's personal effectiveness in the classroom.

It is difficult to use words which convey like meanings to others. Especially is this true when the use is restricted to simple phrases of description without accompanying explanation. With reservations concerning its present form, the scale is here reproduced. An attempt will be made to justify the selection of factors of behavior upon which the scale has been built.

RATING SCALE OF THE TEACHER'S PERSONAL EFFECTIVENESS

I. IN GETTING PUPIL RESPONSE

1	2	3	4	5
Teacher—Genuinely interested in pupils as persons; enthusiastic, vital	Teacher—Dynamic and purposeful; interested in pupil effort	Teacher—Varying from direct interest in pupils to obliviousness of pupils	Teacher—More concerned with routine than pupils; unanimated	Teacher—Apathetic, dull; disregarding pupil purposes
Pupils—Wholehearted in response (physical and mental alertness)	Pupils—Responding to teacher most of the time	Pupils—Varying from eager responsiveness to wandering inattentiveness	Pupils—Listless, conforming dully; showing little concern for teacher	Pupils—Ignoring teacher; finding interest in each other; noisy and careless

II. IN CREATING FRIENDLY CLASSROOM ATMOSPHERE

1	2	3	4	5
Teacher—Conversational, friendly, and with a sense of humor; seeing pupil point of view	Teacher—Friendly, with an understanding adult point of view	Teacher—Serious, reserved, and exacting; stirring competitive effort	Teacher—Aloof, "talking down" to pupils; impatient with interruptions or digressions	Teacher—Critical, faultfinding, harsh, definitely unfriendly
Pupils—Meeting teacher naturally and freely (person-to-person relationship)	Pupils—Respectful; obedient, willingly conforming	Pupils—Self-centered, unwilling to share	Pupils—Intolerant, strained, rude to the teacher and each other	Pupils—Sullen, rebellious or deliberately disturbing to each other and teacher

III. IN ESTABLISHING A FEELING OF SECURITY

1	2	3	4	5
Teacher—Encouraging, constructive, stimulating, confidence-inspiring	Teacher—Constructive in guiding pupil effort	Teacher—Overlooking opportunities for "bringing out" weaker pupils	Teacher—Permitting pupils to laugh at mistakes of others or be overly critical	Teacher—Intolerant of mistakes, demanding, critical
Pupils—Willing to try; undisturbed by mistakes; participating generally and with ease	Pupils—Most pupils willingly participating	Pupils—Capable, self-confident pupils monopolizing opportunities; weaker pupils not responding	Pupils—Uncertain; covering up/embarrassment in various ways	Pupils—Afraid to try; self-conscious, restrained; or rebellious

IV. IN EXERTING A STABILIZING INFLUENCE

1	2	3	4	5
Teacher—Equal to varying demands; courteous and poised (voice and manner)	Teacher—Poised but with evident effort	Teacher—Occasionally rushed, impatient and discourteous to pupils	Teacher—Indecisive, uncertain, distracted; torn between several demands	Teacher—Flustered, hurried, rushing; strained, impatient, lacking central purpose
Pupils—Controlling voices; courteous; aware of each other's welfare	Pupils—Generally attentive to own tasks; cooperative with each other and teacher	Pupils—At times undirected; abandoning tasks; easily distracted	Pupils—Impatient with each other; quarrelsome, irritable; lacking purpose	Pupils—Using shrill voices; noisy, blustering, selfish, rude; demanding attention

V. IN INSPIRING ORIGINALITY AND INITIATIVE

1	2	3	4	5
Teacher—Original in manner; ingenious, resourceful	Teacher—Motivating work thru the use of interesting devices and aids	Teacher—Using an habitual procedure; possessing typical classroom mannerisms	Teacher—No variation in language; dull, prosaic	Teacher—Wholly lacking in ability to intrigue pupils
Pupils—Responsive to extent of offering ideas eagerly and with enthusiasm	Pupils—Showing interest and willingness to participate	Pupils—Following in routinized way; showing little initiative	Pupils—Bored-acting, half-hearted; without purpose or direction	Pupils—Wholly apathetic, dull; a prevalent "don't care" attitude

VI. IN DEVELOPING PUPIL SELF-RELIANCE

1	2	3	4	5
Teacher—Entering into pupils' activities without domination; exchanging ideas, encouraging pupil decision	Teacher—Putting, pupils "on their own"; guiding and suggesting	Teacher—Expecting pupils to "try for themselves" but oversolicitous; hovering, protective; unwilling to trust pupil judgment	Teacher—In didactic manner, telling pupils exactly each step to take	Teacher—Apart, removed; giving "long distance" directions; demanding conformity
Pupils—Initiating; suggesting ways and means; solving problems	Pupils—Accepting responsibility in terms of teacher's suggestions	Pupils—Overanxious about results; constantly referring to teacher	Pupils—Relying on teacher; showing little ability to think for themselves; dependent	Pupils—Assuming no responsibility; showing practically no concern for own actions; uncontrolled

In offering such a scale for consideration, the writer does so with the hope that its validity as well as its usefulness may be verified by school administrators and students in the field of education for the teaching profession.

As has been stated before, the teacher in the modern school should be more than a mere tutor, guiding pupils in the acquisition of information. The argument has been advanced again and again that the teacher should be able to direct pupils' growth in such a way that they are learning to take their places in their social world with satisfaction to themselves and to others. This requires that the teacher understand how personal and social satisfactions are acquired. It also presupposes in the teacher an adult willingness and ability to become instrumental in creating an environment conducive to satisfying activity on the part of pupils. The teacher's part in getting pupil response, in creating a friendly classroom atmosphere, in establishing a feeling of security, in exerting a stabilizing influence, in inspiring originality and initiative, and in developing pupil self-reliance will be dependent upon a working understanding of the needs of the growing child.

The teacher should know and permit to function the basic and instinctive behavior urges of growing children; namely, the organic or physiological needs, the social needs, and the self-expressional needs. For example, the teacher should know that internal physiological processes may impel children to vigorous action which will be offset with bodily fatigue over which they have no control. Likewise the teacher should understand that every child possesses an innate tendency to seek the approval of others, that it is part of his heritage to want the recognition of those with whom he associates. Nor should the ego needs of the individual be ignored. From infancy the child has learned to manipulate, to vocalize, to express pleasure and pain.

He has come to know that he has a self and to assert himself as a person. He requires a growing sense of self-confidence and self-understanding.

The teacher should recognize the outward signs of impelling inner urges and know that the body functions as a whole. When children are all "keyed up" for action, when there is physical readiness for action, there is also emotional and mental readiness. The teacher with insight into the ways in which the bodily organism functions knows that when there is readiness for action, it is disturbing to the entire mechanism to obstruct action. Thwarting physical activity at that particular time brings forth outward evidences of the inner disturbance. These outward evidences may be in emotional outbursts of one kind or another or in some form of tensing of the muscles which shows itself in a variety of ways. The wise teacher furthers rather than blocks these urges to action. The younger the child, the more transparent will be his conduct. He has not learned to "hide his feelings" but usually gives vent to them. The discerning teacher will know that it is far wiser to mold in accord with the natural urges than it is to inhibit them.

The physiological needs are those relating to the proper functioning of the body. The intake of food and rest, conditions of bodily comfort and relaxation, contribute directly to the complete efficiency of the body. Children who are undernourished, fatigued, or whose rate of metabolism is not right do not have the same energy potential as those whose intake of energy is more adequate. The status of each child's vitality is dependent upon proper food, rest, and bodily functioning. The alert teacher will consider this physical well-being in trying to supplement each child's out-of-school life with whatever balancing properties are needed in school. A carefully planned program of activity and rest will be arranged, and each child will be urged or helped to relax according to his physical status and prevailing bodily tone. The observant teacher will temper his voice and manner to meet pupils' physical conditions. He will stimulate the physically less active and try to conserve the energy of the child who dissipates his energy, thereby depleting his reserve. The observant teacher will be alert to corrective needs and make allowances for physical variations in children, but will try always to stir pupils to a physical responsiveness in keeping with their respective physical potentials.

The social needs of children will be the particular concern of the teacher. The classroom is essentially a natural social situation for children. Nowhere else do most children have the opportunity of associating with as many children of their own age as they do in school. The farseeing teacher will try to make the classroom a place in which each individual's effort is respected so that each feels secure in expressing himself. The teacher's encouragement and approval of that which is tried for the first time will in all probability stir the classmates of the one venturing to expressions of approbation. The teacher's careful planning will eliminate the overweighting of chances for failure and will assist pupils to successful accomplishment.

Closely associated with the social needs are the personal or egoistic needs. Every individual grows into a person whose behavior is shaped by meeting the demands of his environment. Each learns to act in relation to a developing life motif or pattern; that is, he acquires habitual ways of responding. He may face facts directly, or he may learn to temper facts to favor his own feeling of security and importance. The teacher who realizes how normal it is for children to blame disturbing consequences of their own conduct upon other people or upon inanimate objects will try to help them face the facts by making outcomes seem as normal as the causing conduct. Instead of penalizing children for mistakes, the idea of making mistakes will be made to be a matter of course by the teacher. By encouraging pupils to exert their initiative, helping them to expect at the start that things may not turn out as expected, the teacher can build up an attitude of willingness to try and to take the consequences whatever they may be. The habit of avoiding reality may be supplanted by a growing habit of accepting reality. The more objective the child becomes about himself, the less tendency there is for him to resort to introspection and misleading opinions about himself.

The teacher who has a consistent influence in developing children's expanding ability to get along happily with other people will not be the teacher who deliberately makes things easy for them. Learning results only through practicing that which is to be learned. Children should not be taught to avoid challenges but to face them without prejudice and without emotional upset. The teacher who loses poise and direction in the face of conflicting demands will not be an example of what he would have children become. The teacher's own behavior either has a stabilizing influence upon children or incites them to similar lack of self-control. An emotionally disturbed state in the teacher contributes directly to a generally disturbed classroom atmosphere.

It is highly important that a teacher be alert, not only to children's needs, but to his own. It is to be expected that children will not have the perspective to see themselves impersonally or through the eyes of another. It is to be expected that the teacher will be able to do this. If the teacher has not learned to evaluate his own conduct or to be sufficiently sensitive to the way in which he affects others, he needs the assistance of one who can help him interpret his own behavior. The foregoing scale is suggested as a means of evaluating the teacher's personal effectiveness in stimulating pupil conduct. This scale is not intended as an all-inclusive measure of a teacher but as an instrument to be used by an observer in recording the pupil behavior which the teacher is instrumental in eliciting.

In using the scale several observations should be made. The majority of pupils in the classroom should be observed rather than the minority or few exceptions. The observer should use the scale only after he is certain that the teacher and class are behaving as they do habitually and not under strain because of his presence.

A scale which considers the interacting behavior of teacher and pupils is not sufficiently comprehensive to make a complete evaluation of teaching. It is suggested that this scale be used in addition to others which are generally used. The writer has worked out this scale because of the fundamental nature of teacher-pupil relationships and because few attempts have been made to specify or describe the kind of behavior which is foundational to personally satisfying and socially worth-while living. Too often the items included in teacher-rating scales deal with abstractions. The rater can record his ratings from a remembered general impression. The scale does not cause the rater to observe systematically children's reactions to the teacher and to watch for any evidences of the children's maturing behavior.

Education's aims are broader today than formerly. The schools of America have been dedicated to the promotion of the human welfare of all members of the democracy. A democracy places its faith in the value of every human being and in respect for personality. The only way in which the classrooms of America may be made into social laboratories for the promotion of improved social conduct and social well-being is to focus attention upon the part the teacher plays in helping children to become persons who know how to work effectively with others for the welfare of all.

Too many rating scales still glorify the academic accomplishments of the teachers. While the school will always need to be the interpreter of the social heritage, it should not neglect consideration of what is happening to pupils while they are learning about what has happened and what is likely to happen. The curriculum of the school has been liberalized to include the arts. Emphasis has been placed upon learning through doing. Yet the great majority of rating scales overlook, in their items for evaluating teaching, the effect of the impact of the teacher's personality upon the immediate behavior of pupils. More general practice of evaluating the effect of adult teaching personalities upon children's conduct should add impetus to the

other attempts which have been made to have education conceived of as a vital ongoing procedure which
is valuable in and of itself for its immediate as well
as for its more remote results.

CHAPTER VIII

IMPLICATIONS FOR TEACHER EDUCATION AND TEACHER SELECTION

This study of teacher-pupil relationships has implications for those who aspire to be teachers and for those who have the responsibility for selecting candidates for teacher preparation and for teaching positions. The fact that the teacher exerts a direct and immediately observable influence upon pupils makes it imperative, if the findings of this study are given credence, to place more emphasis on the candidate's personal influence on children than is customary in most institutions preparing teachers. This is not a new thought. The significance of the personal behavior of the teacher has not been underestimated in years gone by. With present conditions of life, however, there are increased demands being made upon the teacher as a person. More teachers must be helped to meet these demands if the kind of pupil development previously outlined is to be fostered.

The teacher of today should be a person who through percept and through personal stimulus causes children to react in such a manner as to promote their personal well-being and their social usefulness. There is but one way to ascertain a teacher's effect upon pupils. That is discovered by watching pupils' behavior when in contact with the teacher. Intelligence, insight, social understanding, breadth of information, and a studentlike attitude are all indications of potential teaching strength, but they do not give a complex index of a teacher's power. Even the candidate's personal appeal to adults cannot be taken as absolute assurance of success. The real test comes when the prospective teacher is placed in a situation involving direct contact with children. The way in which the children react to the teacher, day after day, is the true measure of the teacher's effectiveness.

The most dependable factor to date for predicting teaching success has been the grade earned by the student in his practice teaching. Other measures which have been given consideration are intelligence, academic accomplishment, and tested understanding of the theory of teaching and learning. Little significant correlation has been found to exist between teaching success and any predictive measure other than between practice teaching and teaching itself. This substantiates the point being made; namely, that the personal stimulus value of the teacher should not be neglected in estimating teaching success.

If we assume that education has two main purposes, the fostering of the mental, physical, and emotional well-being of the individual and the promotion of a democratic social order in which every individual has opportunity to live freely and fully within self-accepted limitations of restraint, we have a frame of reference for general educational goals in which are encompassed the objectives for every classroom. The teacher should be considered successful to the extent to which he contributes to the personal development of his pupils and assists them in acquiring the skills and attitudes essential to adequate participation in a democratic social order.

What then are the implications for the aspiring teacher and for those who are helping to select worthy applicants? They are the same for both. No one should be considered ready to teach nor consider himself a teacher until the effect of his personality upon pupils has been determined. Theoretical knowledge about growth and development is helpful but it alone will not suffice. An ability to interest and direct one or two or even a dozen children may be an indication of effectiveness, but it is not convincing evidence. Since children in large groups affect each other and stimulate each other to behavior different from their conduct when in small groups, teaching thirty or more pupils differs from teaching four or five. An understanding of subject matter and of the psychology of teaching and of learning are indispensable but in and of themselves do not make a teacher. When all is said and done, there is no short cut to absolute certainty regarding teaching effectiveness which should be substituted for actual contact with a classroom full of pupils. Results speak for themselves. Much discouragement to young people preparing for teaching could be avoided and immeasurable improvement made in teaching if every teacher-preparing institution would include as its deciding measure for teaching readiness a student's observed success in affecting in pupils desirable behavior.

Students would be saved time and expense if, before intensive preparation for teaching were begun, the student was required to demonstrate his ability to get along harmoniously and constructively with children. While it could not be expected that he could be held responsible for particularized learning prior to his preparation for teaching, he should be expected to prove his compatability with children. His ability to enter into pupils' activities with understanding and with enthusiasm should be investigated. During the time when the student is acquiring a good liberal-arts background, even before any professional study is begun, the possible effectiveness of his teaching personality might be estimated. The estimate would be an unrefined measure and not comparable with later observations, made during supervised practice teaching, but it would serve as a screening process for separating those students whose personalities are predominately negative in their response-getting qualities.

Since teacher-pupil behavior is one very dependable index of teaching success or failure, those charged with the responsibility for selecting teachers might require some evidence of demonstrated ability to inspire wholesome pupil conduct. If institutions preparing teachers fail to incorporate into the preparatory period a test of personal effectiveness, employing superintendents may serve the cause of youth by insisting upon an apprenticeship time during which the teacher is judged especially upon the reactions of pupils and secondarily upon teaching methods. Young teachers should be expected to be in a learning stage because of their inexperience, but they should show some recognizable signs of being able to stimulate pupils in directions herein outlined.

The previous chapters of this book contain lists of teacher characteristics which beget wholesome results in pupil behavior. Samples of both teacher and pupil behavior have been included which should have implications for teachers in service and for those about to teach. A suggested rating scale has been included which those who are rating teachers may find useful in evaluating some of the more essential aspects of wholesome teacher-pupil relationships. Little has been said up to this point, however, which will be of immediate help to the student who wishes to expand his personal adequacy for teaching. The study of teacher-pupil relationships has some implications for him.

Although by the time the young person has reached college his patterns of behavior are well established, there are some activities in which he can participate which may increase his personal assets. Whatever helps to give him a true picture of himself in his relations with other persons will be of direct assistance. Whatever helps him to understand the problems of others and to see "eye to eye" with others will improve his chances for teaching success. Whatever helps the student to meet problems with poise and assurance and to adjust without emotional upset will serve him well in fulfilling the demands which will be made upon him as a teacher.

The regular academic courses of the college and the extracurricular life which the college affords are designed for this very purpose. These may or may not make the desired contribution to the student's personal development. If they do, it will be because the student is ready to profit by them.

The young teacher needs to form the habit of watching the interactions of personalities. He needs to realize that in every particular contact between individuals the learned behavior of each is being confronted by a relatively new challenge. He will profit by watching the outward signs attendant upon the adjustment of personalities to each other. He will improve his opportunities for guiding others if he will try deliberately to make his own behavior complement rather than oppose the behavior of others.

Another way to grow into a readiness for teaching will be for the student to watch children at play, trying to predict and later to analyze their relations to each other. This will require the watching of the same children again and again in an attempt to establish cause-and-effect behavior results. The student should learn, by regular practice, to become observant of the specifics of behavior. He should try to form his own conclusions and then to compare his observations with the deductions of others, utilizing to the full his knowledge of psychology. Some skill in predicting children's reactions will thus be acquired, and theories concerning behavior and behavior tendencies will take on added meaning.

Nothing will contribute more to an improved relationship with others than the habit of seeing oneself without bias and prejudice and in as objective a fashion as is possible. The prospective teacher should survey his own actions and reactions, considering his possible responses to children's behavior. He should consistently try to place himself mentally in direct contact with children as he sees them at play and as he has observed them in classrooms and in their organized groups. He can well afford to project himself imaginatively into a playground group of excited children and question his own probable mode of behavior. The young person who would make teaching his career cannot know too much about children. He may study the psychology of childhood, he may watch successful teachers in their guidance of children's activities, and he may appraise the motives that give rise to their conduct. He will not know, however, his own personal effect upon children until he sees their own reactions to him.

Teaching is essentially a matter of relationships. Aids and materials enter into the relationships, but in the final sense learning depends upon the stimulating character of the relationship between persons. The eager pupil is usually inspired and impelled to action by the influence of a dynamic teacher. For this reason the sooner the prospective teacher can come to know the part which he can personally fulfill in the teaching equation, the better appraisal will he make of his potential teaching ability.

While scholarship and academic background are important and necessary, the personal stimulus power of the teacher is an essential which cannot be overlooked. Children affect adults and cause them to react in much the same way as they influence the behavior of children. An adult may be quite a different person in a group of adults than when in the presence of children. The immaturity of the children may cause the adult to become patronizing or to assume a childishness which is unappreciated by the children. The intensity of children's activity may cause an otherwise controlled adult to become completely frustrated. Likewise children's relative lack of insight may be wholly uninspiring to an intelligent adult, causing him to be quite dull and apathetic in his responses.

The college student who is contemplating teaching can test and improve his ability to adjust to others of his own age by participating in the life of the college and in the social life of his immediate community.

Knowing how to work with others is a real asset. First-hand experience with the problems of group life is invaluable. Participation in social and civic affairs is broadening. Since teaching is a social calling which demands the services of a socially intelligent and socially alert individual, working and playing with adults contribute essential social perspective and outlook. College experience in and of itself should result in increased personal and social flexibility.

Fortunately institutions preparing teachers have realized the necessity for broadening their curricula. These institutions have assumed the responsibility for providing a rich liberal-arts background as a base for later professional specialization. Most institutions also have campus schools or adjacent city or town schools for affording teaching candidates opportunities to test their ability to teach children. There is every reason to think that the oncoming generation of teachers is acquiring an increasingly broadened cultural and professional teaching background. There is a growing national consciousness among educators that the schools of the nation are the bulwark of democracy, and that teachers play a leading role in social improvement.

There is still a tendency, however, for the college to accept any young person for teaching preparation who scholastically qualifies for entrance. It is uncommon for the prospective teacher to be given an early appraisal of his personal effectiveness in guiding those of the age level he expects to teach. Many discerning directors of student teachers are cognizant of a student's aptitude in this respect during the latter part of his college years. Seldom, however, does an institution have as detailed observational records of a prospective teacher's effectiveness as those contained in Chapter III even upon the completion of professional preparation. Early professional specialization is not advocated. It is suggested, however, that the findings of this study imply that a fraction of the number of certificated persons should never have been encouraged to teach. Colleges need to exert more discernment in not permitting individuals with little or no personal aptitude for teaching to become directed toward a teaching career. An early assaying of personal aptitude might well be made.

Education is being accepted generally as the best assurance for the extension of democratic living. If education is to make this contribution, it becomes imperative that teachers be selected whose teaching is conducive to learnings consistent with democratic principles. Teachers must be endowed with the same attitudes and habits which they would impress upon others. It is economically wise, therefore, both to the young person who desires to teach as well as to society for the candidate's influence upon children to be determined with thoroughness before he is permitted to enter the profession. It becomes the obligation of educators to place the stamp of approval only upon such young people as exemplify the qualities essential for

satisfying living in a democracy. This will require a
real testing of the influence of a prospective teacher
upon pupils and an impartial appraisal of the findings.
Careful scrutiny of the observed influence of the aspiring teacher upon the behavior of pupils gives promise of assured selection and preparation of persons
whose proved behavior exemplifies personal and social
living at its best.

APPENDIX

GROUP ONE

Senior students in the San Francisco State Teachers College, located in San Francisco, California, all of whom had had one year of student teaching prior to the time of filling out the questionnaire. Their teaching experience had been in the campus school of the San Francisco State Teachers College and in selected schools in San Francisco or the cities of the San Francisco Bay region, Oakland, Berkeley, or Alameda. Group One was selected because it included extremely young teachers, whose experience in the classroom as students was still a reality and whose contact with carefully selected "master teachers" and teachers' college supervisors was likewise a present experience.

GROUP TWO

A summer-school class in the San Francisco State Teachers College Summer School consisting of teachers, principals, and supervisors from various parts of California, particularly the San Francisco Bay region. Group Two was chosen because it included teachers, principals, and supervisors of cities and rural sections of California. These teachers at the time of answering the questionnaire were members of a summer-school class studying progressive educational practices.

Group Three

Teachers from schools in New Haven, Connecticut, used as demonstration schools for the State Normal School located in New Haven. Group Three was selected because it included teachers capable of demonstrating good teaching procedure to normal students of the state of Connecticut.

Group Four

Teachers of the West Middle District School of Hartford, Connecticut. Group Four was invited to participate because it included teachers who had been guided by supervisors of outstanding ability and training.

The four groups were selected because of their geographical location, representing the extreme eastern and western sections of the United States. These limited groups were not selected as representative opinion of the country at large but rather as groups composed of teachers who had given some thought to the type of reaction sought and sufficiently separated geographically to indicate whether any regional tendency for teachers to think in particular terms existed.